Everyday Mindfulness

Everyday Mindfulness

From Chaos To Calm
In A Crazy World

Holly Duckworth, CAE, CMP

Everyday Mindfulness:
From Chaos To Calm In A Crazy World
Published by Ione Publishing
Denver Colorado

ISBN: 13: 978-1-7320198-2-9

Self Help/ Devotional/ Leadership

QUANTITY PURCHASES: Schools, companies, professional groups, clubs, and other organizations may qualify for special terms when ordering quantities of this title. For information, email holly@hollyduckworth.com

This book is printed in the United States of America

Introduction

"Life is a daring adventure or nothing."
~ Helen Keller

We live in a world of bigger, better, faster, and more. A world where "okay" really means: I am losing my shit, but I don't want you to know. We live in a world where human doing is rewarded and human being is punished.

Our world, as it is, is unsustainable. We are burning out our people in the frenetic 24/7 world of news and social media. Each week, it seems the headlines present the news of another school shooting, a celebrity suicide, or a dip or spike in the stock market. The ups and downs, like ocean waves, may be a natural phenomena, or they may be the rising of a collective consciousness that says, "Enough is enough!"

Why I wrote this book

Honestly, I wrote this book for me. I needed a place to share the solutions I had found to the day-in day-out challeges of these transformational times. Let me say that another way. I needed a tool to get me through the shit show, and I thought you might need one also.

Oh and, if you host a show called www.EverydayMindfulnessShow.com and you release a show once per week. Does it not stand to reason you would write a book to support your listeners, fans, and coaching clients everyday of the year? I say, "Yes".

How to use this book

We all have the same 24 hours in a day. How we choose to spend them can vary from person to person. Some get up early; others sleep late. For this reason, I see this book as a customizable tool for you. If you are a morning person, use this as your daily go-to for centering and peace. Perhaps you are coffee table person, or need a little pick-me-up to read at the doctors office.

Everyday Mindfulness: From Chaos To Calm In A Crazy World

While this is written with an intention, a quote or affirmation, and a journaling question for each day, it's meant to be about the pauses in between. When you pick up or see the the book, remember that you choose how you spend your days. Spend them wisely.

Each day, you will find three tools to support you in your mindful practice:

- Space to pause and set your intention
- An inspirational quote or affirmation relating to the focus for that day
- A mindful message from my heart to yours

How Do You Become Mindful?

How do you get past the freak out stage to living today? Practice. Yes, you read that correctly. This book is about a commitment to your personal practice of being your honest best self.

Being mindful starts with you exploring your own definition and committing to the open willingness to explore, discover, wander, and refine you and who you are with each page.

You let go of mindless by focusing on the present moment. Now is the only moment you have. What you choose to do in any one moment is how you live your life. It is in the collection of these moments that you build a life. That life, and the energy it represents, becomes your legacy.

As a keynote speaker, author, and trendsetter in the field of mindfulness, I have discovered and rely on a few key concepts:

How you do one thing is how you do everything.

What is mine to do today? And remember, it's not all yours to do.

Stare fear in the eye and go forward, anyway.

Living and leading your life from mindfulness is not a flip switch. It's not a quick fix. Mindfulness is a practice, not a perfect.

Are you ready to accept your human-ness, honor your being-ness, and step into a new way to look, feel, sense, and experience life? Then keep reading.

Opening Commitment

This is the year I recognize my gifts and talents.

This is the year I allow myself to be one with the good I see in my family, friends, and colleagues.

This is the year I realize life not only can be different, but it must be different so that I can have the life that is waiting for me.

This is the year I acknowledge my self value and worth.

This is the year I give thanksgiving every day in every way for all the people, places, things, and experiences that make me my best me.

This is the year I release busy for productive.

This is the year I release worry and fear for surrender and trust.

This is the year I practice being present to what is celebrated each and every moment.

This is my personal commitment to a year of mindful living.

January

Back to Basics

Each month, we will have a focus and theme to help grow our mindful living practice. Think of this as a way to create a synergy with each day. They say it takes 21 days to change a habit, so each month is full of chances to practice these changes. The theme for January is back to basics. This is the choice to go back to the center of love.

I particularly like this definition of mindfulness by John Kabat Zinn: Mindfulness is the practice of being present in the moment with non-judgement.

My expertise is in the area of applied mindfulness. I work with individuals and companies to bring mindfulness to their world. I wrote this book to give you the opportunity to set your daily intention for what you want to happen each day. This will be followed by a quote or affirmation to focus you on that intention and a few thoughts to shift your energy and inspire you to mindfully approach each day.

January 01

My intention for today is

____

____

Intention & Attention

"Our intention creates our reality." ~ Wayne Dyer

Intention is your energy in motion as you begin this new day. And each day forward, you will be asked, "What is your intention for this day?" People have different definitions of intention. I invite you to use the one that is right for you. For some, an intention may be like a "to do." For me, it is not something to do; it is how I choose to show up energetically each day. Place your word, or short statement, in the upper corner of each daily page. Use this word or statement to ground you more mindfully throughout the day. Whatever you focus on increases. When you desire to move from chaos to calm using this book, you will choose calm each day.

Here are a few examples to get you started:

Happy	Beautiful
Kind	Hope
Courageous	Patience
Thoughtful	Nice
Love	Faith

Excited	Focus
Balanced	Grace
Determined	Peace
Brave	Worthy

Each day, as you practice your mindful living and mindful leadership, begin with your intention before your daily task list, using the place on each page to write your intention down. While I do recommend you select positive words, there may be a time and place to set a negative intention. For example, my intention this day is to reduce chaos, or let go of concern. I recommend positive intentions, as what you focus on increases. You could state those negative intentions another way such as increase ease or tranquility. Your words matter. Living mindfully means honoring the up days and the down days. You may wish to flag this page to come back to it periodically for sample words to guide your daily intention-setting practice. Where you put your intention and attention, you will experience growth.

January 02

My intention for today is

____

____

Words of Affirmation

"Do not talk different; act on it." ~ Holly Duckworth

As we move into this new year, we are often flooded with ways to create vision boards or songs or statements of what we want that year to be about. Often, those may be forgotten before the end of the week. This year, give yourself a mindful break. Allow yourself to move with the ebbs and flows of life. Read each daily quote and feel it as your truth in that moment. Use my brief thoughts to help you activate the positive truth of that quote in each day.

Today, make this the day you do not talk about change; instead, you act differently. What is one thing you can do differently to make your life different this year? What is one thing you will become this year to make your life different and better?

January 03

My intention for today is

____

____

Hope For Happier

"Hope smiles from the threshold of the year to come, whispering it will be happier…." ~ Alfred Lord Tennyson

As you mindfully, consciously build your day, week, and year ahead, the choice is yours. Do you choose to be chaotic or calm? Each day, you build upon that choice in your intention setting. Making a daily commitment to your mindfulness practice will make you happier, healthier, and bring hope to a world that needs it so much.

January 04

My intention for today is

____

____

Mindfully Find Your Center

"We resonate with one another's sorrows because we are interconnected. Being whole and simultaneously part of a larger whole, we can change the world simply by changing ourselves. If I become a center of love and kindness in this moment, then in a perhaps small but hardly insignificant way, the world now has a nucleus of love and kindness it lacked the moment before. This benefits me and it benefits others." ~ Jon Kabat-Zinn

Mindfulness is the practice of becoming present every day. Centering is the process of bringing your focus, your energy, to the center of your body. Centering is one skill that builds upon itself. The more you can be still even one minute at a time each day, the more centered you will be in the stressful moments. When you have a moment of feeling off balance, breathe and center yourself.

There you have it, centering – your one simple secret to reduce stress today. Give it a try. Let me know how it works for you.

January 05

My intention for today is

____

____

It Is Done Unto You As You Believe

"Our beliefs control our bodies, our minds, and thus our lives..." ~ Bruce H. Lipton

Beliefs are the lenses that you use to determine what makes you alive. Today, pause and look at the lenses that shape your life. What do you believe about the person you are? Are you good, kind, generous? Or are you stuck, angry, alone? There is no right or wrong, but simply a belief. Is what you currently believe what you want to believe? If not, make a choice to change.

January 06

....

My intention for today is

____

____

Choose Mindful Energy Use

"I don't need to feed my crazy by looking at other people's crazy." ~ Neen James

When you first roll out of bed, is your phone the first thing you touch? How many times each day do you check your social media feed? Mindful living is the invitation to set boundaries about what you post and read...and when. It is scientifically proven that we feed off each other's energy. This is both in terms of the technology we take in and our physical real-life energy. Today, pause for a moment. How does the energy of a room change when you walk into it? Do you want the room to feel lighter? Or, if you are honest with yourself, does a room feel heavier when you walk in? Energy can be craziness, or calm. Today, be mindful of how you feed the world your energy. Be mindful of the energy you give and take in. Choose wisely.

January 07

My intention for today is

____

____

Everything New

"Bring it on, everything new, everything different, everything true. I am ready for my next thing to do."
~ Daniel Nahmod

I'll never forget it. It was January 1, 2011. I was sitting in a chair at my favorite spiritual place. The song Everything New from Daniel Nahmod came on, and I wept uncontrollably. It hit me in an instant. If I was not happy with my life, it was my work to change it. It was time to declare that everything would be new.

We are now a week into the year. How are you feeling about your visions, intentions, or dreams? Where in your life do you wish for something new? That year, everything changed for me. I hope you will use this book to set your daily intentions and move in the direction of what you want, creating a life that is everything you dream of, everything new.

As we celebrate the first week of this new year, it is a good time to gain clarity on what we want to become in the year ahead – to confirm that it is in alignment with the plans we have put into place. Is there something you need to release for something new to come in? What new thing do you intend to have happen for you this year. Bring it on, everything new.

January 08

My intention for today is

____

____

Mindfulness Is Your Choice Each Day

"Every day brings new choices." ~ Martha Beck

Thank you for participating in this daily reader. You have successfully completed the first week of your journey to mindfulness. Each day, you are invited to make a new choice, set a new intention, and apply your mindfulness work out in the "real" world. Be the calm you want to create.

January 09

My intention for today is

____

____

Movement & Non-movement

"We do not stop exercising because we grow old – we grow old because we stop exercising."
~ Kenneth Cooper

Mindfulness does not mean you must be still. Often, people confuse mindfulness with meditation. While meditation can be one form of mindfulness, it is not the only one. Meditation is meditation, and mindfulness is mindfulness. Listen to your intuition, that still small voice inside you. Is it craving to move? Are you listening? Take a few moments to balance your times of movement and non-movement. Even just a few moments of movement such as walking, dancing, or stretching your body can help move your mind.

January 10

My intention for today is

____

____

Gratitude

"Gratitude drives happiness.
Happiness boosts productivity
productivity reveals mastery
and mastery inspires the world."
~ Robin Sharma

What you are grateful for expands. A mindful person is mindful of all the gifts in their lives. Make a list of what you are grateful for. Now look at the list. Are all the things outside of yourself? Now I invite you to make a second list. What are you grateful for about you? Celebrating you and being grateful for you increases your self worth, your self empowerment, and your mindfulness.

January 11

My intention for today is

____

____

Tap Into Your Inner Voice

"The bottom line is that if we want to live a happier, healthier, and more prosperous life, all we need to do is 'shift' our intentions, 'ask' for help, and 'pay attention' to the answer." ~ J.D. Messenger

We live in a world that craves answers. Our world tells us to find a problem and solve it. Living mindfully invites us to look at what we believe and turn it on its head. What if your real strength was not having the answer, but asking a question, asking for help? Today, look at your intention. How can you ask your intuition a question, and then listen? Respond to that voice, that answer, today.

Sample questions:
What can I do that is most loving for myself today?
What is my focus for this day?

January 12

My intention for today is

____

____

Ready, Fire, Aim

"The most important key to achieving great success is to decide upon your goal and launch, get started, take action, move." ~ Brian Tracy

You don't shoot a gun, then aim. You line up, find a target, and then shoot. This year, what is your target? At the start of any year, it is too easy for us to set a goal and then forget it. Or not set a goal and rapid fire into the year. As I look back at the years when I have had my best success personally and professionally, they are the years I have taken the time to get clear on my goals. Yes, the goals may change and adapt, but having a goal or a vision board gives you something to move toward.

January 13

•••••••••••••••••••••••

My intention for today is

____

____

Accept & Allow

"Radical Acceptance is the willingness to experience ourselves and our lives as it is." ~ Tara Brach

As you step into this day, what are you allowing in your life? Too often, we do not actually possess the things we want in our lives because we wish for them, hope for them, and desire them. But once they come into our lives, we put the brakes on. Today, radically accept what you are experiencing in your life. If this life does not make you happy, then ask yourself what new thing, experience, person will you allow to come in to change your life.

January 14

My intention for today is

____

____

Imagine Life in Alignment

"When you are in alignment with the desires of your heart, things have a way of working out."
~ Iyanla Vanzant

Where in your life are you experiencing stress and discomfort? Relationships? Finances? Health? This will be the place where you are most out of alignment with the "heaven on Earth" you are here to create. Where are you feeling joy, ease, and comfort? The places of joy are places of alignment. Today, let go of one thing not in alignment and accept one thing that makes you feel more alive.

January 15

••••••••••••••••••••••

My intention for today is

____

____

Choose Well

"There is no passion to be found playing small – in settling for a life that is less than the one you are capable of living." ~ Nelson Mandela

From time to time, we all come across people who say, "Who do you think you are?" Okay, maybe they don't even say it, they simply make us feel it. These well-meaning people, underneath it all, may be jealous. They are wishing, hoping, and dreaming they could live the stress-free, mindful life you have chosen. Honor your connection to Spirit and live the life you have imagined regardless of others. If a naysayer crosses your path, thank them, bless them, and let them live the life they have chosen. Tip your cap to what you are cap-able of being. There is no big or small life, only the life you have chosen.

January 16

My intention for today is

____

____

Live Possibility

"May you be filled with loving kindness.
May you be well.
May you be peaceful and at ease.
May you be happy."
~ Anonymous

In a world that tells us each day of madness, fear, chaos, and loss, you have a choice. Will you stay in the light of possibility or succumb to the world that speaks of anger, ego, and challenge? Use this quote as your mantra today: I am filled with loving kindness. I am well. I am at peace. I am at ease.

Can you help navigate any dark people, places, or things you may encounter this day? Live YOUR possibility. Stay positive!

January 17

My intention for today is

____

____

Make the Movie Of Your Life

"Maturity includes the recognition that no one is going to see anything in us that we don't see in ourselves. Stop waiting for a producer. Produce yourself."
~ Marianne Williamson

The world loves going to movies as an escape from "reality." When was the last time you went to a movie, or had one on digital download in your home? Living mindfully can cause us to want to escape. This work is simple, but not always easy. Today, come back to yourself. If you were making the movie of your life (and you are): What movie would you make? Who would play you? What makes your movie a best seller? Produce your movie, starting today.

January 18

My intention for today is

____

____

Value You & Value Your Relationships

"Your life is a series of relationships. The higher the percentage of High-Value Relationships, the greater your prospects for success. Turn each of your relationships into a High-Value Relationship." ~ Jim Cathcart

It is said you are the sum total of the five people closest to you. Who are those people? As a child, I remember hearing the song, "Make new friends, but keep the old; one is silver and the other gold." In today's globally connected world, it is technologically easier to connect to and hang onto friends who may be of less value. Yet, what I have learned living mindfully is that letting go of relationships that no longer serve me or the other people can be healing. This January, go back to basics. Who will you keep in your life this year? Who will you let go? Value you and where you invest your relationship energy.

January 19

My intention for today is

____

____

Play

"Life is the ultimate game, let's play!" ~ John Chen

When we were children, we lived to play. That childlike wonder helped us to connect, learn, and grow. As adults, we create systems that fill our time and keep us away from play. Today, take a moment to play.

Simple playful suggestions:

Go swing in a nearby park
Rent a bike and go for a ride
Download and color a coloring page from the internet

January 20

My intention for today is

____

____

Change Happens

"Be the change you want to see in the world."
~ Mahatma Gandhi

No doubt, in this moment you have a "to do" list of things you must do, of change you want to see happen. As you look at this list, do you feel like it is work or a cause to be overwhelmed and feel pain, or do you feel like it has opportunities to be full of joy. Often, my readers are neutral to negative about the work they do and the change they are here to create. Inspired by the words found above, be the change. How will your day be different by approaching your "to do" list positively, finding joy in the change you are here to make?

January 21

My intention for today is

____

____

Inspiration and Perspiration

"Sometimes when things are falling apart, they may actually be falling into place." ~ Amy Steinberg

As we mindfully vision each day of this year, it's easy to have a "plan" for how we desire our life to fall into place. One powerful mindful practice is to surrender to how your life is in the moment. Flow with the moments that inspire you, accept the moments that make you sweat, and trust that your life in every moment is falling into place.

January 22

My intention for today is

____

____

This Little Light of Mine

"You don't need to find the light, you ARE the light; and when you let your personality shine you can light up the world." ~ Sally Hogshead

A few years ago I traveled to Bali. On the trip, we did volunteer work in one of the schools for young girls. As we were driving up, the host asked me if I would share a skill or talent with the women. Instant panic! What could I share that would help them? Immediately, I went to my inner voice, and asked what talent I could give that would benefit them. The answer my "inner voice" sent back was to sing. What? I am far from a singer. Sing the song, "This Little Light of Mine." As you get to know me, you will discover that I don't just talk mindfulness, I live it. I took the stage with the women and began to teach them the song. I would soon learn they already knew it. We sang the song together. The room lit up. No matter where you go this day across the street, country, or world, as you look across the boardroom, at the car next to you at a stoplight, or in the mirror: Remember to let your light shine in the world.

January 23

My intention for today is

____

____

Recognize

"We know there is intention and purpose in the universe, because there is intention and purpose in us."
~ George Bernard Shaw

In affirmative prayer, the prayer modality I teach and share, the first part of the process is to recognize the good all around us and within us. This month as you return to basics, look around you and see, feel, sense, and know all the good all around you. That good you see outside is the same good in you.

January 24

My intention for today is

____

____

Seek the Star You Are

"We cannot fight the Universe. It refuses to be budged from Its course. We can only go with It."
~ Ernest Holmes

Each day flows without efforting. The sun rises, the rivers flow, the flowers grow. Are you in alignment with that flow? Today, choose to be in alignment with what happens for you, not to you. Observe, as good becomes your reality. Look up and be the star that you are.

January 25

My intention for today is

____

____

Realize

"The real voyage of discovery consists not in seeking new landscapes, but in having new eyes."
~ Marcel Proust

Our eyes are the windows to the world. We often become robotic in what we see each day. We get up in the same bedrooms and drive the same cars on the same routes to the same jobs to do the same work, only to return to the same houses. We look from the same eyes each day. Today, what would happen if you mindfully chose to see with new eyes? Could you look in a new direction? Today, move a piece of art in your home. Maybe drive a different way to work. See yourself and your work in a new way. Consider having new eyes. Awaken to a new self discovery.

January 26

My intention for today is

____

____

Accept Your Best

"Good, better, best. Never let it rest. 'Til your good is better and better best." ~ St. Jerome

Back to Basics month is almost over. What is your "auto-pilot" inner voice saying to you? Are you building yourself up with self talk or accepting less than your best? Each day, we are only asked to create ourselves a little better than the day before. Today, look at what your best was yesterday in whatever role you chose. Ask yourself how you can be one percent better and do that; become that today.

January 27

My intention for today is

____

____

Minimalism

"The more you let go. The more you rise." ~ Unknown

One of the best memories I have with my mother, and there are lots of them, was the day I took her up in a hot air balloon. What we learned that day was that we had to "let go" of what we thought being in a hot air balloon would be to have the full experience of flying above the trees with the greatest of ease. What thoughts, beliefs, or actions are you holding onto today? Can you let one go and rise a little more to your greatness?

January 28

My intention for today is

____

____

Gratitude vs. Appreciation

"Happiness cannot be traveled to, owned, earned, worn, or consumed. Happiness is the spiritual experience of living every minute with love, grace, and gratitude."
~ Denis Waitley

Words...we use them so casually nowadays. We throw them around with an email, tweet, or text, assuming that both sender and receiver get the same message. While there are more ways, and words, to communicate now, the messages are often more jumbled. There is a lot of talk about being grateful. Writing a gratitude list each day is great practice. Do it.

Today, I want to also highlight appreciation. When was the last time you paused to appreciate, recognize, understand, or acknowledge a person, place, or situation that supported you on your path? Today, write an expression of gratitude and take a moment to appreciate the feeling of kindness and appreciation expanding in your world.

January 29

. . . .

My intention for today is

____

____

Opportunity & Paradox

"Life is an opportunity, benefit from it.
Life is beauty, admire it.
Life is a dream, realize it.
Life is a challenge, meet it.
Life is a duty, complete it.
Life is a game, play it.
Life is a promise, fulfill it.
Life is sorrow, overcome it.
Life is a song, sing it.
Life is a tragedy, confront it.
Life is an adventure, dare it.
Life is luck, make it.
Life is too precious, do not destroy it.
Life is life, fight for it."
~ Mother Teresa

Funny how sometimes life contradicts itself. Instead of being frustrated or confused by it, accept life on life's terms. Practice mindful living – being present in what is, no matter what that is.

January 30

My intention for today is

____

____

Grab Your Map & GPS

"Your goals are the road maps that guide you and show you what is possible for your life." ~ Les Brown

I sometimes think about what life was like when we had to use "real" paper maps to go places, when we didn't have the voice of our GPS to guide us. I'm told you would map out a destination and not veer too much from it. If the map said take Route 12, you took Route 12, even if that guided you through traffic.

I am grateful to know Karen Jacobsen, the original voice of the GPS. I like to think of GPS as code for Good Positioning System. When I asked her what word or question she gets asked to repeat most often, it is of course the familiar "re-calculating." As you gain tools for mindful living, keep your map and GPS handy. The possibilities to re-calculate are always expanding for your life.

January 31

My intention for today is

____

____

Attracting or Pushing

"At all times, we are either drawing things to us or pushing them away." ~ Ernest Holmes

Today, as you spend time in your mindfulness practice, ask yourself, "What is it I truly desire?" Am I inviting that energy in or pushing it away? When you press the gas and the brakes of your car at the same time, you spin out. Where are you spinning out in life? Is today the day you stop pushing and start attracting?

February

Centering in Self Love

Resistance is futile! The collective awareness of the planet in February is that of love. For the purposes of this month's applied mindfulness practice, I want you to center into self love.

February 01

My intention for today is

____

____

Self Awareness Inside

"What lies behind us and what lies before us are small matters compared to what lies within us."
~ Ralph Waldo Emerson

Each day we get up, brush our teeth, do our hair, and get dressed. Our world has conditioned us to focus on our outside looks. Today, pause and look within. What lies within you is the most important part of you. Go within and ask yourself what your best qualities are. Celebrate them, and celebrate you this day and throughout this month of love.

February 02

....

My intention for today is

____

____

Faith of Love

"Be with your loved one in wholeness, acceptance and wonder. In the presence of love, everyone gets what they need in their own language." ~ Tama Kieves

We have more tools to communicate today than we have ever had before. Yet, we are the worst at communicating with one another. The pace of life is filled with moments of joy and celebration, coupled with fear and sadness. In the chaos, we often do not know what to say, so we say nothing. We do not know what to do, so we do nothing. Today, remember the faith of your love. Reach out to someone and share your presence and support. That same gift will be returned to you by faith.

February 03

My intention for today is

____

____

Belief in Love's Power

"One of the most spiritual things you can do is embrace your humanity. Connect with those around you today. Say, "I love you," "I'm sorry," "I appreciate you," "I'm proud of you"...whatever you're feeling. Send random texts, write a cute note, embrace your truth and share it...cause a smile today for someone else...and give plenty of hugs."~ Steve Maraboli

Today, remember you are a human being, not a human doing. Wherever your path takes you this day, center back into your humanbeing-ness. Be mindful in how you are sharing your energy with the world. Are you the man or woman always in a hurry, rushing to the next thing? That energy is what people feel when they are with you. As you read this today, return to your belief in love. Mindfully carry the energy of love with you wherever you go today.

February 04

My intention for today is

____

____

Bold Boundaries to Self Love

"Daring to set boundaries is about having the courage to love ourselves even when we risk disappointing others."
~ Brene Brown

No. Did you know that the word no is a complete sentence? It is. One way to practice self love is to set boundaries. Today, and every day, I invite you to make choices that choose you. Say "yes" when you feel the "yes." Say "no" when you feel the "no." These boundaries are healthy. Anyone who honors a boundary will soon learn a no is a yes to something else wonderful. It is never about the other person or project. It's simply a yes to you.

February 05

My intention for today is

____

____

Potential of Love

"Love goes very far beyond the physical person of the beloved. It finds its deepest meaning in his spiritual being, his inner self. Whether or not he is actually present, whether or not he is still alive at all, ceases somehow to be of importance." ~ Viktor E. Frankl

The human body is wired for survival. We don't have to think about breathing or living; we naturally breathe, and from that breath we take in life. Holocaust survivor Viktor Frankl so eloquently lived love even from the darkest depth of a concentration camp. His life showed us how inner strength is naturally potent love that has its being within us. No matter what challenge or opportunity you face this day, lean in to love. Love is your essence, potential, and power. In love, you find meaning.

February 06

....

My intention for today is

____

____

Dynamic Living of Love

"An awake heart is like a sky that pours light." ~ Hafiz

February is the month of love. We are surrounded by little cut-out hearts and candy hearts; boxes of chocolates seem to appear out of thin air. While a heart for some is merely a shape, for others it is a body part. A mindful person is invited to look at his or heart as an engine. Today, close your eyes and breathe in love, breathe out love. Put your focus and attention into your heart center and feel it awaken just a little bit more.

February 07

My intention for today is

____

____

Love and Forgiveness

"I've learned that people will forget what you said, people will forget what you did, but people will never forget how you made them feel." ~ Maya Angelou

Recall a moment in your life when you felt upset at someone, maybe even very mad. A time that you were wronged. Got one. What did you do to overcome that emotion? As I coach clients, I have learned that the answer is forgive. Forgiveness as a mindful term is never about the other person. It is always about you. Today, accept yourself, bless yourself, and forgive yourself for the situation you just recalled and any other scenario you may be in now. Forgiveness is not forgetting, but bringing power to live and let live.

February 08

My intention for today is

____

____

Hope for Yourself

"A leader is a dealer in hope." ~ Napoleon Bonaparte

I believe everyone everywhere is a leader. That leading is not a role or position, but a state of mind. This day, what do you hope for yourself and the world? What will you do today as a leader to make your hopes come alive?

February 09

My intention for today is

____

____

I Am All In For Love

"If you want a life worth remembering, when you are asked to do something adventurous and you have time and money, there is only one answer: 'I'm IN!'"
~ Tom Morrison

Today, what will you choose? Will you sit on the sidelines of life or ask, "Put me in, Coach." There are some people who always sit on the sidelines of life. Others dive in. We only get one life, so make the most of it. Find something today you have always wanted to see or do, and you have take one step in the direction of experiencing that life adventure. It's not a game unless you put your hand up and ask to be "put in."

February 10

My intention for today is

____

____

Soul Pursuits

"Be relentless in pursuit of what sets your soul on fire."
~ Unknown

At time, words become acronyms for me. That is the case with the world S.O.U.L. I translate it to Sacred Openness to Universal Source. Today, open yourself to all things being possible. In your meditation or quiet time, mindfully focus on keeping your mind, heart, and hands open to receive the good that the Universe is trying to give to you.

February 11

. . . .

My intention for today is

____

____

Let Love Transform You

"If you change the way you look at things, the things you look at change." ~ Wayne Dyer

This quote always makes me smile. How is it possible that people can look out the same window and one will see joy while the other sees sadness? Today, as you look around your world, focus on seeing the good, beauty, and joy. Ask a few people around you what they see. Focus on the good. Let your world change.

February 12

My intention for today is

____

____

Turning Love Knots into Why-Nots

"Love makes intellectual pretzels of us all, I think."
~ Einstein

Where in your life are you knotted up? Often, we run through life so fast that we don't realize there are blockages and stoppages. Where do you turn into a pretzel to please others? You only have one job in this life – to do your work with joy. Where is it that you pretzel unnecessarily for someone else? Today, love what you have created and turn your pretzel into a French loaf of bread. Straight and simple.

February 13

My intention for today is

____

____

Learn Again

"Love is what we were born with. Fear is what we learned here." ~ Marianne Williamson

I love watching young children play on a schoolyard or playground. They often have no rules of right or wrong, good or bad. They simply play. As each year as the school of life goes by, they begin to learn who the "good kids" are and who are the "bad ones." Our world starts in love and teaches us fear. Today, learn to love again.

February 14

My intention for today is

____

____

Love as a Way of Living

"Be so filled with love, there is no room for anything else." ~ Unknown

Valentine's Day. Did you know that Hallmark sells more than 20 billion dollars in Valentine's Day cards each year? And the American Retail Federation estimates only 55 percent of the population actually celebrates. It's interesting how love has become a retail holiday. Today, fill your heart with the feeling of love. Pause, breathe, and let yourself love yourself. Look in the mirror, state an affirmation, make a list of 14 things you love, and appreciate yourself.

February 15

My intention for today is

____

____

Worthiness & Weariness

"Our job is to love others without stopping to inquire whether or not they are worthy." ~ Thomas Merton

My name is Holly Duckworth. It's not lost on me – my name even makes me worthy. Now I get that not everyone can have my name. And you are reading this book and applying mindfulness to your life; therefore, you too are worthy. As a child on this planet you are worthy of good, growth, love, joy, and all good things. Stop asking if you are worthy. Stop looking for permission to be worthy. By the power vested in me, I say: stop ducking your worth, and accept your worthiness. See it? Duckworth. I declare you worthy.

February 16

My intention for today is

____

____

Overcoming Love's Obstacles

"People think a soul mate is your perfect fit, and thats what everyone wants. But a true soul mate is a mirror, the person who shows you everything that is holding you back, the person who brings you to your own attention so you can change your life." ~ Elizabeth Gilbert

February brings the world's awareness to love – where it is, and where it is not. Some even call Valentine's Day "Singles Awareness Day." This month, know your perfect everything. Stop holding yourself back. Bring attention to what you love about you. From that place, you will change your life.

February 17

My intention for today is

____

____

Synchronizing Love

"Let the beauty we love be what we do." ~ Rumi

Offering to serve others, helping, and working with others is a beautiful thing – no matter what your job, whether parenthood, retail, construction, executive, in the medical or legal field. Today, look around and see the beauty in all you do. Give thanks for it.

February 18

My intention for today is

____

____

I Realize

"I'm ready to be who I came here to be.
Each step brings me closer to free.
I realize
I realize
All inside of me."
~ Laura Berman

To realize is to become aware. Some may think you grow quiet in meditation during a deepening mindfulness practice. Applied mindfulness is what we are working on. The purpose is to help you realize that your entire life can be mindful. Today, realize the joy, peace, sadness, frustration, good, and bad inside of you. When you are aware, you free yourself from it. Go be who you came here to be.

February 19

My intention for today is

____

____

Courageous Self Love

"One thing is for sure — you will make mistakes. Learn to learn from them. Learn to apologize. Learn to forgive yourself. Learn to laugh when it all comes down because, sometimes, it will." ~ Vironika Tugaleva

I'm a perfectionist; maybe you are, too. Even as I type this, I know my words are powerful. I know that whatever follows the words "I Am" creates my reality. Today, use "I Am" and learn. I am learning. I am apologizing. I am forgiving. Be willing to live from the center of your heart. Have the courage to be imperfect. In that place is your power.

February 20

My intention for today is

____

____

Connecting to Love's Promise

"There's no substitute for a great love who says, 'No matter what's wrong with you, you're welcome at this table.'" ~ Tom Hanks

Growing up there were few rules in our house. One of them was that everyone was welcome at our table. Our house was often the house where people from around the neighborhood would land. These gatherings always gave us opportunities to experience new people, places, and ideas. Who can you welcome at your table today?

February 21

My intention for today is

____

____

Love Body, Mind, and Spirit

"During your times of trial and suffering, when you see only one set of footprints, it was then that I carried you."
~ Footprints

My favorite place to be is the beach – which is funny now because I live in the land-locked state of Colorado. When I do make a coast or beach visit, I love watching the waves gently wash away footprints. Today, give thanks and remember you don't have to walk this journey alone. We walk it with the support of the Universe carrying us exactly where it wants us to go.

February 22

My intention for today is

____

____

Feeling Love Healing

"And now these three remain: faith, hope, and love. But the greatest of these is love." ~ The Bible

I gave great consideration to the choice whether to include religious text in this book. While I am a student of world religion, I recognize that you, my reader, may not be. I do not believe in excluding any religion or faith tradition. I believe we all have wounds to heal from our upbringing, religious or not. Whatever your case is, today concentrate your focus on faith, hope, and love.

February 23

My intention for today is

____

____

How Deep Can You Go

"Be great today, wherever you stand." ~ Anonymous

Each word has purpose and meaning:
Be – I exist, therefore I matter
Great – Regardless of circumstance, there's an opportunity to be above normal
Today – Keeps me focused on the present, with no thoughts of yesterday or tomorrow
Wherever – Wherever I am, both mentally and physically
You – Could easily be the word "I," it helps me focus internally
Stand – Whether I'm at the top of my game and setting a personal best or struggling to find the strength to go forward, there's something about the word stand that tells me no matter the circumstance, I will be upright with purpose

February 24

My intention for today is

____

____

Feminine & Masculine

"The union of feminine and masculine energies within the individual is the basic of all creation."
~ Shakti Gawain

As a young girl, I often wore oversized t-shirts and no makeup. This experience taught me at a young age the art of being neutral. Don't be too sexy. Don't show up like a boy. In our commercial world, we see photoshopped women (and men) all around us. Today is your invitation to meld the masculine and the feminine. We are the union of the both. Look at your energy and celebrate the masculine qualities that help you show up in the world. Honor the feminine ones that give you empathy and compassion. Our world is expanding its definitions of gender. Love your both, no matter what gender you identify with.

February 25

My intention for today is

____

____

Forget What Is, See What It Could Be!

"I find that seeing everyday things for what they are … rocks, trees, ice formations, fences, etc. … and then imagining what else they suggest if seen as metaphors, often opens the door to insights, thoughts and feelings lurking in our minds." ~ Dick Durrance

Look and listen to the world around you with awe and reverence. Look beyond the form of tree, rock, fence. What do you see just under that label? Today, find an object that catches your attention. Commune with it. Ask it to reveal to you the truth it wants you to uniquely see.

February 26

My intention for today is

____

____

Begin Again

"Argue for your limitations and sure enough they're yours." ~ Richard Bach

I hear it from clients every day: I don't have enough time. I don't have the right skills. I can't do this mindfulness thing; my monkey mind always wins. You can't live in both a limited and an unlimited world. It is either limited, or all things are possible. Today, look at where you are setting a self-limiting belief. Stop it.

February 27

My intention for today is

____

____

Poof! Voila!

"When you love all of yourself, as if by magic, you will find yourself being completely loved by others."
~ Katie & Gay Hendricks

In the classic story, with the wave of her fairy godmother's wand, Cinderella is transported to her new life with her prince. What if that fairy godmother was a metaphor for the good, the God, of life all around us. Wave the magic wand of your intention this day, say "Poof! Voila!" and let your love fuel the love around you.

February 28

My intention for today is

____

____

Evolving Love's Promise

"The promise of evolving love is to use whatever comes up as an opportunity to heal past wounds, to understand our partners more intimately, and to remove any obstacles within ourselves to experiencing love's full depth."
~ Carl Studna

We live in a world of instant gratification. Right now, you can order groceries and have them delivered to your home in two hours. You can order packages and have them delivered the next day. Everyday mindfulness moves from chaos to calm. Is now the time to calm down and evolve? Some of the best things in life come through time. A glass of wine, cheese, even friendships sometime take time to age, and they often get better with age and experience. Today, look your life and celebrate the places where love is evolving and growing.

February 29

My intention for today is

____

____

It's All Alright

"Everything will be alright in the end. If it is not alright, then it is not the end." ~ Unknown

So many times in life we awfulize. Awfulize means that we start thinking of all the things that can go wrong and don't spend enough time thinking about the things that can go right. Today, catch yourself when you go down the path of awfulizing and choose to tell yourself a new story in which everything is alright.

March

Going Beyond Your Current Beliefs

May these quotes and mindful moments invite you to examine your past beliefs, honor your current beliefs, and choose your future beliefs.

March 01

My intention for today is

____

____

Beliefs Fuel Your Life

"You become what you believe." ~ Oprah Winfrey

When I present as a keynote speaker, I often have my audiences break down the word believe. By re-arranging the letters, you can get to be-a-live. What is fueling your life today? Is it the belief that you have to "do something"? Or the belief you are here to "become something"? Today, ask yourself what you be-a-live about life. Listen for your answer.

March 02

My intention for today is

____

____

World Day of Prayer

"Prayer does not change God, but it changes him who prays." ~ Soren Kierkegard

I did not grow up in a house that prayed. Heck, I did not grow up in a "Bible" house at all. So when I was licensed as a prayer practitioner through Centers for Spiritual Living, my family was a little surprised. It really doesn't matter if you choose to pray or not to pray, you are supported in that choice. On World Day of Prayer, remember that you can't pray wrong. Some will ask for things in prayer, others will affirm what they know to be true, some will simply say, "thank you." Today, make your day itself a prayer.

March 03

••••••••••••••••••••••••

My intention for today is

____

____

Believe & Achieve

"When the voice and vision on the inside is more profound, and more clear and loud than all opinions on the outside, you've begun to master your life."
~ John DeMartini

When coaching my clients, I often find I pause for a very long time before answering a question. Sometimes, it takes a moment longer to go within, to sort through the files of my heart and the data in my mind to locate an answer. This skill is cultivated by doing my own inner work. Today, go one step closer to mastering your own life. Listen to that voice within, and turn up the volume.

March 04

My intention for today is

____

____

March Forth Into Your Value

"Try not to become a man of success, but a man of value." ~ Albert Einstein

It's come to my attention that we live in a value meal world. At almost any place you go, there is a choice of package A, package B, or package C. As a rule breaker, I often want part of package A, a bit of package C, at the price of package B. I see value in all of it. (Okay, maybe not the pickles.) Where do you see your own value? As our humanness craves success, remember that your value is found in seeking and sharing your value with the world. You don't have to make it hard – what's your value you give to the world?

March 05

....

My intention for today is

____

____

Decide & Make A Difference

"What you do makes a difference, and you have to decide what kind of difference you want to make."
~ Jane Goodall

Our world needs everyone single of us. There is no big or small in jobs. No more or less in contributions. Today, ask your heart what difference it is here to make. Accept your particular difference a little more each day. Find a way to contribute that difference. We don't remember the whole of life; we remember the difference each person made here on Earth.

March 06

My intention for today is

____

____

Future Fulfilled by Belief

"Your present state of mind influences your future status and money." ~ Raj Setty

Where are you with your state of mind about money? That mind creates your emotions and the world you live in. As you look at your checkbook or financial records on this day, what story are you telling? Create the future you want with the words and stories about money that you tell.

March 07

My intention for today is

____

____

Evolve

"Our beliefs evolve." ~ Vishen Lakhiani

Society today asks us at a young age,"What are you going to be when you grow up?" What was your answer? Did you evolve your beliefs, thoughts, and actions to become that? There is no right or wrong. Today, slip into the childlike wonder of what you would believe and do if you could evolve to be that thing you secretly dreamed of being as a kid, or even dream of today as an adult. Evolve.

March 08

My intention for today is

____

____

International Women's Day

"Well-behaved women seldom make history."
~ Laurel Thatcher Ulrich

Mindfulness is choosing what fills your mind and dumping the rest. We choose what rules we want to accept and what rules we do not. As a result of these choices, we live the consequences and the opportunities. On International Women's Day, how will you use this one day to make history? Even the smallest act can ripple out good for men and women around the world.

March 09

••••••••••••••••••••••••

My intention for today is

____

____

Exactly Where I AM

"i am exactly where i need to be
i need to be exactly where i am
i am a blessing manifest."
~ Amy Steinberg

We only have now. No matter how much we future-ize or history-ize, we have now. Today, pause and know you are exactly where you need to be. Bless that truth.

March 10

My intention for today is

____

____

Believe in the Power of Hope

"I am not what happened to me, I am what I choose to become." ~ Carl Jung

Sadly, too many people have childhood experiences, or even adult experiences, that are less than loving. You don't have to look far to hear of terrible things happening around the world. Yet, we survive on the shared knowledge that we can become something new each day. Today, take one step to becoming what you dream you could be.

March 11

My intention for today is

____

____

Believe in Present Possibilities

"What would it be like if I could accept life – accept this moment – exactly as it is?" ~ Tara Brach

Breathe in acceptance. Breathe out fear. Breathe in acceptance. Breathe out fear. There is a wisdom in you that knows the answer to this question for you. Ask it. Where and what do you need to accept life as it is in this moment?

March 12

My intention for today is

____

____

Imagine Your Beliefs into Becoming

"Worry is the ego hijacking the imagination"
~ Justin Foster

When I see the word "ego," I see something very different than many other people do. I see the acronym Expanding God (Good) Opportunities. Today (and everyday), you get to choose. Will your ego cause you worry and fear, holding back what you imagine? Or is today the day you re-frame your ego and invite it to help your imagination? Imagine what you can become with the shift of this powerful word.

March 13

My intention for today is

____

____

Be YOU! Be FASCINATING!

"You don't have to change who you are, you have to become more of who you are." ~ Sally Hogshead

The definition of fascinating is being extremely interesting. Sally Hogshead's work mathematically helps you find where you are fascinating and helps you activate it in your world. Check out her work online. What if your life was not about becoming what a parent or teacher told you to become but was the process of becoming your best self? They say the average person now has seven or more careers. Along the journey, you often have to become one thing to have the skills, talents, and abilities to become the next, and then the next. What can you do today to be more interesting? How can you become interested just a little more in others?

March 02

My intention for today is

____

____

Define Mindfulness

One beautiful thing about mindful living is there is no one agreed-upon definition of mindfulness. And there are fewer definitions on how to apply mindfulness.

mind·ful·ness

the quality or state of being conscious or aware of something.

a mental state achieved by focusing one's awareness on the present moment, while calmly acknowledging and accepting one's feelings, thoughts, and bodily sensations, used as a therapeutic technique.

Today, consider your own definition of mindfulness. Lean and grow into that with your practice each day.

March 15

My intention for today is

____

____

Seek to Understand

"We refuse to believe that which we don't understand."
~ Napoleon Hill

We simply cannot know everything. Research, data, and information is being created at millions of bytes per second. We can only seek to understand and surround ourself with the people and tools that get us to the right information at the right time to do our right and perfect work. Note: in that statement, I put people first. Today, don't get so caught up in technology that you forget how conversations with real people can help you believe and understand life in new ways beyond a web search, website, or app.

March 16

My intention for today is

____

____

New View, New Beliefs

"A desk is a dangerous place from which to view the world." ~ John Le Carre

I've always had a "desk job." However, that desk is almost never in the same place two days in a row. No matter what your job, whether you work in a home office, retail space, office tower, or on a construction site, change up your view today. Be willing to look at your work from a new angle. If you think that's impossible, then just for fun, go sit at someone else's desk for a minute. Get a new perspective on something you may take for granted.

March 17

My intention for today is

____

____

Open the Door to Blessings

"May your troubles be less and your blessings be more and nothing but happiness come thru your door."
~ Irish Blessing

There is all this talk in the world today about diversity and inclusion. The more I read, study, and experience, the more I come to the conclusion that we all, at the end of the day, want the same things – peace, blessings, and happiness. Today, be the happiness that walks through every door.

March 18

My intention for today is

____

____

March Into the Inevitable

"At first, dreams seem impossible, then improbable, and eventually inevitable." ~ Christopher Reeve

You are the super-man (or woman) in your life. Knowing this, what is your dream, your wish? Today, select one thing you dream you could do, be, have, or become. Put on your cape, and march one step in the direction of your dream.

March 19

My intention for today is

____

____

Do!

"It doesn't matter what you say you believe – it only matters what you do." ~ Robert Fulghum

All you ever need to know you learned in kindergarten. Share. Wash your hands. Live a balanced life. Look back on the rules you have established yourself. Are they serving and supporting you or holding you back? What do you need to do today to align what you learned early on in your life with what you want in your life today?

March 20

• •

My intention for today is

____

____

Take a Stand

"If you don't stand for something, you will fall for anything." ~ Gordon A. Eadie

Life is a series of tradeoffs. You make one person happy, you may make another one unhappy. And we must take a stand for something. Today, make a list of those things you believe in so deeply that you will stand for them.

March 21

My intention for today is

____

____

Begin With Beliefs

"Your present circumstances don't determine where you can go; they merely determine where you start."
~ Nido Qubein

I had the honor of meeting Nido Qubein several years back on Martin Luther King Day. He invited me as a guest to see the campus of High Point University. It was indeed a high point of my career. Why? Because Nido is not merely all the titles he has earned, but is the man who invites others to start where they are and grow the life, love, empire they want to create. Nido came to this country with few dollars and few connections but has expanded them to create one of the best institutions for learning in the U.S. Start where you are. Determine where you want to go. Leverage your dollars and connections, and you too will create high points in your life.

March 22

. . . .

My intention for today is

____

____

Own You!

"Maybe it is not what you don't know; it's what you do know but don't own." ~ Darren LaCroix

Read this quote today carefully. In fact, read it a few times. It is a quote by the 2001 International Toastmaster of the Year.

Which of your traits do you not own? Today is the day. Own it. Own you. Go out and use that skill to make the world a better place.

March 23

My intention for today is

____

____

Success Is Assured

"Success is most often achieved by those who don't know that failure is inevitable." ~ Coco Chanel

Success is a direct result of your own self confidence and belief in yourself. Today, make a list of 10 things you know are positive and true about yourself.

March 24

. . . .

My intention for today is

____

____

The Wisdom of Pooh

"You're braver than you believe,
stronger than you seem,
and smarter than you think."
~ A. A. Milne

Most of our beliefs were founded in our childhood. What was your favorite book or song as a child? What was the lesson that book instilled in you? Today, as you adventure into the world, believe you are brave and smart.

March 25

My intention for today is

____

____

Live Your Faith

"Faith is about doing. You are how you act, not just how you believe." ~ Mitch Albom

This book has many, many quotes about the power of belief. Living a mindful, spiritual life can also be about balancing your doing and your believing. You can't spend all your days in meditation and expect to fully live your faith. You can't spend all your time out doing and feel faith flow through you. Today, balance your belief and your faith.

March 26

My intention for today is

____

____

Expand From Your Heart

"Life shrinks or expands in proportion with one's courage." ~ Anaïs Nin

When I started my business back in 2010, I wish someone would have shown me that graph of business success. You know, the real one. Not the line we dream of where the growth is just a natural upward incline. The real one where the line goes up, then down, then up again. This is true not only for my business, but for my mindfulness practice, too. Some days it goes up, other days it goes down. It takes courage to expand and courage to contract. Today, honor all the expansion and contraction of life as you feel your lungs naturally expand and contract. It's natural. It's good.

March 27

••••••••••••••••••••••

My intention for today is

____

____

Amazing Things

You will do amazing things with the choices that each day brings. And with every step you take, bless the progress that you make.

"The reason you live is there in every gift
love your life, love your dreams
you will do amazing things."
~ Michael Gott

Throughout this book, I feature lyrics from a positive music singer songwriter. Music can be a tool for emotions in ways that words and journaling cannot. In his song, Michael Gott reminds us we will do amazing things. Today, don't minimize the work you do. Look around, and look at the amazing things you are. Bless the progress you have made.

March 28

My intention for today is

____

____

It's A Practice, Not A Perfect

"Believing takes practice." ~ Madeleine L'Engle

Mindful living every day is part art, part science – but mostly it is practice. Mindfulness is repetition. Our human brains are programmed to create a plan and execute on the plan. Becoming more mindful requires us to make the plan, then surrender it. Surrender over and over again. Each and every day, by using this book and applying mindfulness in "real" life, you give yourself an opportunity to practice. Believing, as we spoke about earlier, is be-a-live. Today, practice believing in your aliveness.

March 29

• •

My intention for today is

____

____

One Step At A Time

"Believe you can and you're halfway there. "
~ Theodore Roosevelt

Mindful practices can sometimes be lonely. Choosing to be the person who says, "I will not live in chaos, I choose calm," can often make you feel like a salmon swimming upstream. Whatever it is you want in your life – money, friends, career, health – feel into the belief that it is already a part of your life. As you swim in the new direction of your life, your belief in what is possible expands. Look around today and find someone who has what you desire. Remember that when you see it in others, you can make it your own. I trust you are already on your way to what you desire.

March 30

My intention for today is

____

____

Spirit Never Fails

"Success is not the absence of failure; it's the persistence through failure." ~ Aisha Tyler

Life sometimes gives us the opportunity to "reboot." Those times can feel like failure. We have to choose if we are going to re-create the life we once had or if we will totally start over. I am living proof that we survive these reboot moments. Each failure has been a step that I later learned brought me to a new higher and better place. Today, no matter what you are going through, resist the need to label your challenge a failure. Reframe the failure into the opportunity to move to a higher and better place, in whatever way.

March 31

....

My intention for today is

____

____

All People Are Leaders

"In the future, there will be no female leaders. There will be just leaders. " ~ Sheryl Sandberg

I used to tell people that I taught mindfulness to CEOs and executives. I often got a look back like I was crazy. People always assumed my clients were men. Actually, my clients come from all walks of life. And everyone is a leader. You may be leading from a church, a household, an office building, or a city. No matter what, you must choose to be the leader of your own life. Today, pay close attention to your assumptions. Are you assuming that the only leader is the most powerful person in the room? The one in the front of the room? What if that were not true, and you were, too? You lead from the way you show up, grow up, and believe. Act as if you are the leader in your life today.

April

Affirmation

Affirmations are short, positive, present tense statements that capture what you want. It is my hope that your work this month will help you affirm what you want in your life. Instead of inspirational quotes, I offer you an affirmation each day. These words are qualities of good, qualities of God, that inspire and motivate us to change. Your mindset is the beginning of your mindful journey.

To stretch your practice, say these statements up to 70 times each day.

April 01

My intention for today is

____

____

Fun

I am fun!

Happy April Fool's Day – a day where many choose to celebrate childlike wonder and fun. Life is meant to be lighthearted and amusing. Have a little fun today.

April 02

My intention for today is

____

____

Joy

I am joy.

You are what you create your world to be, the stories you tell yourself. We live in a feeling world. Today, give yourself permission to rejoice and to feel happy, glad, and blissful. Today, affirm the joy.

April 03

My intention for today is

____

____

Ease

I am ease.

Despite society's conditioning us to think the opposite, our life is actually not meant to be hard. The best of life is simple, fun, and easy. Today, find one way you can simplify, relieve stress, and make your life easy.

April 04

My intention for today is

____

____

Peace

I am peace.

Let there be peace on earth, and let it begin with me.

Our days are designed to be free and lived in harmony. Repeat this affirmation 70 times to bring more peace to your world.

April 05

My intention for today is

____

____

Kind

I am kind.

Affirmations promote good quality. The statements are simple and have words we often don't hear often. Kind is one of them. Today, spend a moment being kind to yourself. Kindness is our natural character, our essence, and our best way of being. Be more kind, my friend. Today, be more kind.

April 06

My intention for today is

____

____

Light

I am Light.

I love words that have two meanings. As you read and remember today's affirmation, feel yourself getting lighter in terms of both weight and brightness. See yourself turning up the dimmer or flipping the switch of light in your life. Or focus on and feel the lightness of your inside essence.

April 07

My intention for today is

____

____

Worthy

I am worthy.

Believing we are worthy or not worthy is something all of us secretly struggle with. Today, I remind you that there is no one anywhere stamping people with a stamp that says worth or unworthy. We are all worthy simply because we are alive. Today, repeat this affirmation and know you are worthy in every way.

April 08

My intention for today is

____

____

Shine

I am a bright shining light of Love, Spirit, and Service!

You are here to shine the light of your gifts, talents, and experiences in the world. Allow yourself to shine.

April 09

My intention for today is

____

____

Playful

I am playful.

Do you take life too seriously? Some of the most mindful moments are when you become fully present and just play. Give yourself permission today to let the seriousness go and find pleasure in being playful.

April 10

My intention for today is

____

____

Loving

I am loving.

To love is to show you care. There are millions of ways you can show your love today and affirm that you are loving. Open a door for someone, smile, shake a hand, give a hug, whisper good wishes to someone. What you love expands.

April 11

My intention for today is

____

____

Grateful

I am grateful.

If you only say "thank you," may that be enough. Feel appreciation, and show appreciation and kindness. Be grateful for all that you have this day. Start with your body, mind, home, car, and all the things that you may take for granted. The little things do become the big things.

April 12

My intention for today is

____

____

Awake

I am awake, aware, and alive.

One of the most often overlooked gifts is the gift of being alive. To have the opportunity each day to live, breathe, and make a difference. Today is a day to awaken your thinking, to be aware of all the good around you, and to celebrate being alive.

April 13

My intention for today is

____

____

Grace

I am grace.

Every word has the meaning we choose to put upon it. Every affirmation is the same. How do you define grace? How do you align your life with this word and concept? Grace is a rarely used, beautiful word and a feeling energy. Today, be elegant, courteous, and stand with grace.

April 14

My intention for today is

____

____

Healthy

I am healthy.

When was the last time you paid mindful attention to the human bodysuit you get to inhabit in this life? Mindfulness is being aware of your body. Today affirm its health, wellness, and vitality.

April 15

My intention for today is

____

____

Abundant

I am abundant.

The world is plentiful when you choose to see it that way. Abundance is the truth of our world. Prosperity is how you allow that abundance to flow through your life. Today, place your attention on the large quantities of abundant life opportunities you have. Today, you are abundant. Live from that awareness.

April 16

My intention for today is

____

____

Free

I am free.

Today, mindfully release yourself from any place you are putting yourself in confinement, captivity or restraint. Freedom is a state of mind. Open every aspect of your life to receive and give from this awareness of freedom.

April 17

My intention for today is

____

____

Smart

I am smart.

As I write and work with my own daily affirmations, I often find myself at the dictionary to confirm that I am affirming what I truly want. This word, smart, surprised me. Smart is not only a mental intelligence but can refer to speed and appearance. Today, expand your definition of smart. Be of quick wit, dress stylishly. Allow this expanded definition, the combination of the beauty of your brains and Spirit, shine through. That is smart.

April 18

My intention for today is

____

____

Flow

I am flowing.

There is nothing stagnant on this planet and in this life. All things flow. Even the cellular structure of a solid rock is flowing. Breathe in a slow breath, then breathe out. Honor all the things flowing in and out of your body, mind, and life this day.

April 19

My intention for today is

____

____

Comfortable

I am comfortable.

What you think about, you bring about. Today, relax. Find a moment to be unworried. Feel content. Allow yourself to be cozy, warm, and pleasant. In this energy, you will align with your calm.

April 20

My intention for today is

____

____

Wealthy

I am wealthy.

Our world often tells us it is not "okay" to speak of money or wealth. What if all we ever learned was wrong? Wealthy does not just mean money and things. Wealthy is a state of mind and being. Today, feel into the wealth you have and are in money, relationships, emotions.

April 21

My intention for today is

____

____

Renew

I am renewing.

Today, give fresh life and strength to a project you may have set aside. Renew an interest in your life today.

April 22

My intention for today is

____

____

Ethical

I am ethical.

In a world of "right" and "wrong" or "good" and "bad," affirm that you always know what is right in terms of human character. Today, explore your interpersonal words, thoughts, and actions. Affirm that you always make honest, virtuous, and ethical choices. As a mindfulness-practicing person, you set the standard of goodness. Thank you.

April 23

My intention for today is

____

____

Patient

I am patient.

While most of us wear a watch, or watch a clock at the end of each day, we are bound only in the present moment. Mindfully pause and remember the power of patience. Trust that all things are happening on the right timeline. Today, you are patient.

April 24

My intention for today is

____

____

Oneness

I am one with the Earth.

There is only connectedness. As you grow your mindfulness practice, everyday you will continue to see ways people, places, things, and events are connected. Today, feel into your oneness with all the good in the world. This is truth.

April 25

My intention for today is

____

____

Understanding

I am understanding.

Today, pause to feel the dual definition of the word understanding. To be understanding is to have comprehension of a skill – the "know-how." But it is also the adjective of being compassionate, sympathetic, and considerate. From this place of understanding on this day, you live, move, and have your being.

April 26

My intention for today is

____

____

Focused

I am focused.

Our world is a buffet of choices. At times, it is hard to know what to choose to put on your plate. Today, affirm that you are focused on all that you desire and need for your most mindful, stress-free life. As you affirm your focus, more focus and clarity will come to you.

April 27

• •

My intention for today is

____

____

Courage

I am courage.

The choice to practice releasing chaos in this crazy world is a courageous one. As you read each page, you are courageous. Today, honor your ability to live from core heart.

April 28

My intention for today is

____

____

Brave

I am brave.

Life is not always easy. It is in the challenges that we find our brave. What would you do today if you were brave? Do that.

April 29

My intention for today is

____

____

Creative

I am creative.

To be alive is to create. Often, being creative is blended with art to mean being an artist, musician, or author. That is a limited definition of creativity. All of us are creative. Look at your life. Honor what you create whether it is a meal, career, family or more. Today, honor what you create in your life beyond titles and products. Celebrate the energy of joy that you create.

April 30

My intention for today is

____

____

Prosperous

I am prosperous.

Living a mindful life is choosing to be fully in each moment. It is often the choice to let go of society's programming and accept a new path. Prosperity is flourishing financially – to be strong, successful, and in great quantity. Choose to be prosperous now.

May

Meditation, Movement, and Miracles

May the theme for May and quotes on meditation, movement, and miracles help you become mindful about your relationship to your body, mind, and spirit.

May 01

....

My intention for today is

____

____

Mindful in May

"May the sun bring you new energy day by day
May the moon softly restore you by night
May the rain wash away your worries
May the breeze blow new strength into your being
May you walk through all the world and know its beauty all the days of your life."
~ Apache Blessing

Each May, my company renews its commitment to touching one million lives with mindful practices. With this blessing, we remind ourselves of our connection to nature, the beauty of each new day. As you set your intentions this month, may you be reminded of your beauty and the beauty that surrounds you.

May 02

My intention for today is

____

____

Breathe & Receive

"Feelings come and go like clouds in a windy sky. Conscious breathing is my anchor." ~ Thich Nhat Hanh

Do this. Take a moment to breathe in and breathe out. You are in the midst of what can be a busy spring season. As you breathe in, feel your word of intention coming into focus. As you breathe out, feel energy that you don't want departing. When in doubt this day, simply breathe.

May 03

My intention for today is

____

____

New Thoughts Welcome Here

"You never change things by fighting the existing reality. To change something, build a new model that makes the existing model obsolete." ~ R. Buckminster Fuller

It is what it is. That is good news for those of us who like to try to change what is. We can't be children for ever. Seeds must grow into flowers, and the sun must give way to the night. Where do you need to let go of resistance and surrender to a new beginning? New thoughts welcome here. Pause. Breathe. Allow.

May 04

My intention for today is

____

____

Wonder What's Now

"Do you really want to look back on your life and see how wonderful it could have been had you not been afraid to live?" ~ Caroline Myss

Ban regret from your life. I adopted this one rule early in my spiritual and mindful training, and it has has changed how I approach work and personal life. Whenever I am approaching a new person or project, I find myself asking, "If I do not do this, will I regret it?" If the answer is yes, then I go full steam ahead into the experience. Seize the adventure, life won't wait!

May 05

My intention for today is

____

____

Ask & Listen

"Praying is the time to ask, and meditating is the time to listen." ~ Gabrielle Bernstein

In times of chaos when you desire calm more than anything, there is one thing I invite you to do – practice. Practice asking and listening to your intuition within. If this idea makes you uncomfortable, remember that you can't do your practice wrong. Do the practice that works for you. If you pray, pray. If you meditate, meditate. If you simply need to breathe, breathe. Remember the world is for you, never against you.

May 06

....

My intention for today is

____

____

Journey Your Happiness

"It's important to have goals and reach for your dreams, but it's never a reason not to enjoy the present moment. Ultimately it's the journey, not the result, that brings the most happiness." ~ Jessica Ortner

If you have not heard of tapping, this may be a time in your practice to consider googling the concept. Tapping is the process of lightly tapping on your body to awaken, align, and feel safe in your body. People use it to release the old and accept the new. No matter what you want to create for your life – more money, weight loss, love – each day brings you responsibility to journey to what makes you happy.

May 07

My intention for today is

____

____

Self Love Always

"It's not your job to like me, it's mine." ~ Byron Katie

Too often, we go out into the world seeking approval from others. Subconsciously, or consciously, you may be seeking approval from a family member, loved one, or boss. This is not a mindful way to live. Mindful living is the call within to make sure you love yourself. The deeper you love yourself, the more you can be loved by others. Start working on self love today.

May 08

My intention for today is

____

____

Be An Angel On Earth

"Highly successful people attract guardian angels here on Earth." ~ Noah St John

Your life will change the day you look around and recognize that you, and everyone else on the planet, is an angel. We are here to support one another on the journey to live, love, laugh, and be our highest self. Today, be an angel to someone else and allow your angels to show up for you.

May 09

My intention for today is

____

____

Friend The Now

"Make the present moment your friend rather than your enemy because many people live habitually as if the present moment were an obstacle that they need to overcome in order to get to the next moment. And imagine living your whole life like that, where always this moment is never quite right, not good enough because you need to get to the next one. That is continuous stress."
~ Dan Harris

Our world is continuously teaching us that it's better to be busy. If you aren't stressed, there is something wrong with you. I say to those people, "Consider what would happen if doing life that way was wrong." Today, look at your life. Where are you over-programming yourself, co-workers, or family? Is this really what you believe life must be? Take one commitment off your to-do list today, or this week. Watch what happens. You give yourself permission to live a little better, and a little less stressed. And the world goes on just fine. Don't just take my word for it. Try it.

May 10

My intention for today is

____

____

Give It Up

"Giving up doesn't always mean you're weak. Sometimes you're just strong enough to let go." ~ Taylor Swift

A few times a year, I grab the garbage bags and make a donation bag. While not always fun, it's one of the most spiritual, mindful practices I do. I walk through the house and find items that no longer bring me joy. I ask items if they are ready to be released. This practice can be done with both items and people. Giving up a once-cherished item, or person, opens up room for the next thing or someone and room for you to cherish.

May 11

My intention for today is

____

____

Light The Truth

"Separation is an illusion." ~ JD Messenger

How many times do you walk in a room and glance around, and all you see are people different from you? You mindlessly look around and see competition or confrontation. In this moment you are creating separation, whether you know it or not. This quote reminds us that there is no separation. We are all one human family connected irrevocably to one another. As you navigate your day, try to sense where you may be creating separation. And instead choose connectedness. You'll be surprised how good it may feel.

May 12

My intention for today is

____

____

Rebelliously Living Mindfully

"Your body is not a temple, it's an amusement park. Enjoy the ride." ~ Anthony Bourdain

Like everyone else, mindful or spiritual people can become a little uptight about things. I've sometimes been called "holier than thou" by people who don't take the time to take me off a pedestal and get to know me. I selected this quote to remind us that sometimes the finer things in life may not be deemed healthy or normal or in line with the "rules." And more than every once in a while, you need to have fun! Remember, life is a gift to be enjoyed. Today, do something purely for the fun and enjoyment of it. Be a little rebellious.

May 13

My intention for today is

____

____

Stepping Stones to Success

"That which has proved to be a stumbling block to one individual is a stepping stone to a more courageous soul." ~ Cavett Robert

Where have you reached a stuck point in your life or mindfulness practice? Call that into your awareness today. If you were to stop believing this thing were a stumbling block and start to see it as a stepping stone, how would you approach it differently? Today, turn your stumbling block into a stepping stone. Ask for help where needed. Re-arrange the road to go around it. The answer is within. Go there. You got this!

May 14

My intention for today is

____

____

Heart's Longing

"It does not interest me what you do for a living. I want to know what you ache for and if you dare to dream of meeting your heart's longing."
~ Oriah Mountain Dreamer

It may surprise you to learn that I hate networking events. Yes, hate – a word I don't use very often. They are a challenge for me. Everyone shows up with a name, rank, and serial number attempting to meet the next person that will offer to buy what they are selling. It can be awful at times. I really don't care what you do for a living. Today, put your title aside and remember what you long for. What do you desire? Where do you want the world to move as a result of your life?

May 15

My intention for today is

____

____

Storytelling In The Dark

"The confidence that individuals have in their beliefs depends mostly on the quality of the story they can tell about what they see, even if they see little."
~ Daniel Kahneman

Is your life a haunted house or an open meadow? Do you secretly fear that as you walk around the dark hallways of your life, you will come upon a skeleton, vampire, or ghost? Or is your life an open meadow where you see the blue sky each day, enjoy the warm sun on your shoulders, and see a graceful path beckoning you to keep walking? These are only two examples from which you can choose. You may not see far, but what you do see and how you see matters. What story do you tell yourself each day? Make sure you have confidence in the story you have built, are building, and will continue to erect.

May 16

My intention for today is

____

____

Budd-a-ful Now

"Do not dwell in the past, do not dream of the future, concentrate the mind on the present moment."
~ Buddha

Now. Now. Now.
Repeat it with me.
Now. Now. Now.

Anticipatory grief is real. Sadness of the past long gone is real. Yet all we truly have is now. Sit with Buddha this day and allow your mind to empty and your heart to fill. Feel the energy of this now moment where everything you need (food, water, shelter) is provided. All is truly well. Now.

May 17

My intention for today is

____

____

Badass Spirituality

"Surrendering is the free-falling backwards into the unknown and trusting that The Universe will catch you."
~ Jen Sincero

Many people have the misconception that being spiritual is all about being kind, nice, prim and proper. To that I say, "Well, um...yeah…maybe…" Spiritual living is about being who you came here to be, without apology. Then allowing others to become the same. There's nothing wrong with being a badass. Today, what must you surrender to allow the life you came here to live grow a little bigger than you thought it would be?

May 18

My intention for today is

____

____

Non-movement Moves You

"In the midst of movement and chaos, keep stillness inside of you." ~ Deepak Chopra

Let's revisit this book's title – *Everyday Mindfulness: From Chaos To Calm In A Crazy World*. Yes, the world can be chaotic. But you don't have to be. You are what you choose to be. You are what you choose to become each day. Balance your need to move today with your need to be still. Take a pause, as you read, to be still. In stillness, you find success.

May 19

My intention for today is

____

____

You Already Are

"Our job in this lifetime is not to shape ourselves into some ideal we imagine we ought to be, but to find out who we already are and become it." ~ Steven Pressfield

In this quote, I find good, new, and interesting news. Note, I did not say bad news. When you keep asking yourself why you are here, over and over and over again, you keep finding within yourself new answers. Life is your becoming. While your human-ness may say that becoming has to do with a career, today I invite you today to answer the question another way. Try becoming what you already are, your energy.

May 20

My intention for today is

____

____

Keep It Simple

"Feel First. Manifest Second." ~ Andy Dooley

When in doubt and fear, and feeling overwhelmed, keep it simple. Feel what you want to feel. See what you want to see. Just let go of what you don't want to feel, and manifest something new.

May 21

••••••••••••••••••••••••

My intention for today is

____

____

Rebuild or Start Over

"You do not find fulfillment by rearranging the circumstances of your life. You find it by being in touch with who you are at the deepest level and being an express of that in the world." ~ Melli O'Brien

Have you ever had an epiphany? Maybe you prefer to think of it as an "ah ha" moment? A moment when all the lights go on in your mind or heart and you go, "Wow, why didn't I get that a long time ago?" A moment you may simultaneously love and hate. Because you are seeking a stress free life, I'm going to bet you read many books, attend classes, and maybe have a coach or two. Often, we seek to re-boot our life or re-arrange our life with the help of these tools when what we we truly need is to let go and begin again. Wherever you are and whatever you are going through, ask yourself, "Is it time for a re-build or time to start a whole new life?"

May 22

My intention for today is

____

____

Spirituality vs. Religion

"Religion asks you to believe.
Spirituality asks you to look.
Religion has dogma.
Spirituality has wisdom teachings.
Religion wants obedience.
Spirituality wants experimentation.
Religion speaks of sin and hell.
Spirituality speaks of karma.
Religion wants to comfort you.
Spirituality wants to liberate you.
Religion is external. Spirituality is internal.
Religion is the form. Spirituality is the essence.
Religion wants to comfort you.
Spirituality wants to inspire you.
Religion is an institution. Spirituality is a journey."
~ Unknown

Feel into this quote – what does it mean to you? No right. No wrong. No judgement. Sit in the mindfulness of this inspirational writing and find what you believe. Live your day in that centered place.

May 23

My intention for today is

____

____

Reward What You Want To Become

"The highest reward for man's toil is not what he gets for it, but what he becomes by it." ~ John Ruskin

In a world that is always challenging us to become more, it can be easy to covet the person who is or has what we want to become. In creating that energy, we actually repel what we desire. Look today to the people you admire, the people you wish you could be like. Send them thanks for their toil, which can clear the path for you to become what you are here to become.

May 24

My intention for today is

____

____

Vision & Accomplishment

"What you visualize, you actualize." ~ Holly Duckworth

With this new day, you have the opportunity, and the obligation, to visualize what you want to have happen. Do not get caught up in awful-iz-ing. Actualize. Spend a few minutes seeing what you want to happen and sensing that it is actually happening right now. Close your eyes and see the movie of what you want to happen. Everything is twice created: once in your mind, then in form. Create what you want to have happen in your life today.

May 25

My intention for today is

____

____

Scarce No More

"The biggest of our illusions is the trance of scarcity."
~ Dr. Roger Teel

Where in your life are you believing or thinking something is in short supply? Is it money, health, family, or friends? There. Go there. There is where you can begin being mindful today. Shine the light of your energy in that place. Send yourself, and that aspect of life, the truth that there is no scarcity and no lack. Don't deny the balance in your money, health, relationships, or any other aspect of your life. Lean into that aspect and the possibility to grow there. By the power of this quote, be open to begin from that place and see more new prosperous beginnings. Ask for help, and remain open to receiving it. Let go of the trance of scarcity, and open to total Oneness.

May 26

My intention for today is

____

____

Balance Head & Heart

"Science brings knowledge; spirituality brings meaning. We need them both." ~ Unknown

I tend to be an all-in or all-out person. This makes living a mindful life a little tricky sometimes. The present moment can require a shade of grey somewhere in the middle. Where are you stuck and making a black or white decision? Today, invite a little healing. Find a new shade of grey. Be willing to accept balance. Ask for harmony. Become healed.

May 27

My intention for today is

____

____

What Have You Got to Lose? Risk Life

"Death is not the biggest fear we have; our biggest fear is taking the risk to be alive – the risk to be alive and express what we really are." ~ Don Miguel Ruiz

I know some of you will read this and go, "I have a family, job, responsibilities. I can't risk my livelihood for some far-fetched fantasy." And if that's true for you, I can't change that. But risk does not have to be a big thing. It does not have to be a scary thing. Risk is simply a willingness to see things in a different way. Risk may be feeling a new emotion or choosing to respond vs. react. In a recent keynote speech, I told my story about growing up in a trailer park. The story I said I'd never ever ever tell on a stage. I did it. People connected and learned more deeply. I risked. I didn't die. What are you willing to risk? Life is pretty amazing on the other side.

May 28

My intention for today is

____

____

People Please No More

"If you want to live an authentic, meaningful life, you need to master the art of disappointing and upsetting others, hurting feelings, and living with the reality that some people just won't like you. It may not be easy, but it's essential if you want your life to reflect your deepest desires, values, and needs." ~ Cheryl Richardson

Some inspirational quotes are not inspirational the first time you read them. This, for me, is one of them. It's downright painful. Any fellow people pleasers out there? Today, you must start anew with pleasing only one people. That people is you. When you stand for you – centered, calm, and kind – you can say, do, and become things you never thought possible. Use your mindful practice today to set a boundary. Say "no" or say "yes," and while you may not make everyone happy, you make the most important one happy – yourself.

May 29

....

My intention for today is

____

____

Right Thinking, Right Living

"That a man can change himself...and master his own destiny is the conclusion of every mind who is wide-awake to the power of right thought."
~ Christian D. Larson

Do you believe you can change your destiny? In order to do this, you must begin in your mind. Nobody can tell you how to live rightly or how to live wrongly. Only you can do that. Spend a few moments today enjoying the light that you are. Give gratitude for your being awake and for the awakening yet to come. From this, your Right Living is already emerging.

May 30

My intention for today is

____

____

Alternate Living

"Instead of focusing on the world's problems, give your attention and energy to trust, love, abundance, education and peace. :-)" ~ Rhonda Byrne

The timing of this book was no accident. It came to me in a moment of quiet listening, just like those moments I am teaching you to experience. Mindfulness is the practice of being present in the moment with non-judgement. In this moment, center into peace. If your world doesn't feel peaceful, transform your mind to a place where you do feel peace, maybe the ocean or a forest. Turn your attention to educating the world on what you want, not what you don't.

May 31

My intention for today is

____

____

Love Wash Over Me

"Kindness wash over over me. Make me a symphony, play every note you can find…"
~ Gary Lynn Floyd

Do you ever turn on the radio or an online music station and the perfect song is playing for you in that moment? If you mindfully pay attention, you may find that happens more than you are aware. These particular lyrics are on my playlist often. Love wash over me. Everyday mindfulness is the willingness to let love wash over you at home, at work, in the car, at the grocery store. As you navigate your day today, when a moment of chaos comes over you, think back to this reading. Let love wash over you.

June

Intention

How is it possible we have been on this journey for so many months already? Our June theme is intention. By now, you have been writing a short intention each day or considering how you want to put your energy in motion each day. This month, your quotes are designed to keep your intention alive and energized.

June 01

My intention for today is

____

____

Unconditional Living

"You can choose the what, the Universe chooses when."
~ Ravi Tangri

We are exactly halfway through the year. How are you doing with your intentions? Flip through each of the pages. Isn't it exciting to see how your intentions are seeds beginning to grow in your world? Keep focused on what you want to have happen this year. Let the Universe bring you the when.

June 02

My intention for today is

____

____

Wanderlust

"To travel is to live." ~ Hans Christian Andersen

I ask you, what do you believe about travel? Is it an extravagant luxury only for the wealthy or a natural experience open to all? Whatever you believe about travel becomes your reality. When I said yes to travel, I learned more about myself than I would have staying home. Traveling as a solo person, I've been able to laugh as I look for the familiar in a far-off land or just explore the unusual in my own backyard.

Travel is however you define it. Go. Wandering.

June 03

My intention for today is

____

____

Book Knowledge vs. Life Knowledge

"Don't tell me how educated you are, tell me how much you have traveled." ~ The Quran

I love books. Once, a group of friends told me that if they were ever on a game show, I would be the "phone-a-friend" in the category of books. Great. But book knowledge is only as great as how much you apply it. When this quote refers to how much you have "traveled," I invite you to not think of this as going on a trip. Instead, think of it as the broader meaning of traveling the path of life. Today, explore your heart. What is your favorite book? How has it helped you travel your life's path?

June 04

....

My intention for today is

____

____

Tick Tock, Now!

"The mind constantly moves to the past or the future but the reality is this: the point of power is always in the present moment!" ~ Dennis Buttimer

So few people today wear a watch. And if they do, the watch no longer is a timepiece with traditional hands that click and clock around to mark the passing hours. Watching familiar things like this fade away can make me sad. New things like i-watches and digital faces have replaced the old watches with hands. In your life today, look around and see what, like the watch, needs to gently fade away? What new thing can you replace it with? Your power time is now time. Watch what you can create.

June 05

My intention for today is

____

____

Possibilities Abound

"Every adversity, every failure, every heartache carries with it the seed of an equal or greater benefit."
~ Napoleon Hill

I've had a lot of what I now call "bounces" in my life. Some might call them failures. What I have come to know is every "failure" has brought me to something better. It has not always been easy or fun in the transformation process. Yet somehow, it's always better. Today, reflect on your life. Where can you reframe a failure into a bounce? That new story is the seed of your greatness.

June 06

My intention for today is

____

____

Shame Be Gone

"Shame is the most powerful master emotion. It is the fear that we are not good enough." ~ Brene Brown

Over the years, I have had many experiences with friends in 12-step programs. These programs provide places for people to go, dump shame, and be supported by others who are brave enough to admit challenges and imperfections. Where in your life are you telling yourself you are not good enough? Stop the story. Find a friend. One step at a time and you will discover you always were enough.

June 07

My intention for today is

____

____

Question Everything

"Sometimes the questions are complicated and the answers are simple." ~ Dr Seuss

When we were kids, we questioned everything. Why is the sky blue? What do I want to be when I grow up? As we grow older we are trained to have the answers not the questions. Mindful living, reducing your chaos, and creating calm is an invitation to go back to the questions. It's true, some questions are hard – like how do we build a peaceful world? Some are easy –what do I want for lunch today? No matter what, question everything. What you may find is your intuition, your inner voice, just may surprise you with the answers.

June 08

My intention for today is

____

____

Attention Addiction

"The addictive nature of Web browsing can leave you with an attention span of nine seconds—the same as a goldfish." ~ Sally Hogshead

Now that it is already June, you have been practicing mindfulness for some time. Can you feel how you are less addicted to speed and more addicted to slow? You are less addicted to chaos and seeking more calm. Turn the addiction of your attention to what you most desire to have in your life.

June 09

My intention for today is

____

____

Honest Inside & Out

"Peace of mind comes when we exercise our right to be honest, especially with ourselves." ~ Jack Rose

In today's social media world, it's easy to create a regular life and then a Facebook life. Classes in personal branding and how to make yourself "look good" are everywhere. The best life – the truth of life – is that there is, in fact, one life. Be honest with yourself today. Where are you in alignment and being honest? Where are you not? Maybe today is the day to be more honest with you.

June 10

My intention for today is

____

____

Crazy Living

"Good ideas are always crazy till they are not."
~ Elon Musk

I often reminisce about the days when the word Amazon was a river in Africa. Now it's the largest online selling platform in the world. I think of those early days when the Amazon founders must have been called crazy. All great ideas were once crazy. What crazy brilliant idea will you bring into form? Start today.

June 11

My intention for today is

____

____

Perfect Opportunity – Now

"Don't wait for the perfect opportunity. Just take an opportunity and make it as perfect as you can."
~ Mark Sanborn

Life can be full of excuses not to do something. And one reason to do something. Do it because you can. Do big things and little things. Things that make sense and things that make no sense. Your willingesss to expand will make for a mindful amazing life.

June 12

My intention for today is

____

____

Bless Them On The Way

"What other people think of me is none of my business."
~ Wayne Dyer

Oh, the humanity of life. Someone looks at us the wrong way, or says something to us that we don't agree with, and it's so easy to jump into defensive mode. To need to find a way to prove that you are right and they are wrong. Today in your practice, let the words of Wayne Dyer inspire you to honor other's words and thoughts, and then let them go. Trust that what they think of you, and quite frankly what you think of them, is nobody's business. You will attract the people who believe in you, who need what you provide, and you can let the rest go.

June 13

My intention for today is

____

____

Alchemy of Transformation

"We do not need magic to transform our world. We carry all of the power we need inside ourselves already."
~ JK Rowling

Who didn't want to be a magician at some point in their childhood? The Harry Potter books expanded the desire to be a wizard to children for many generations to come. Alchemy is the process of transforming matter into new things. Alchemy, in mindful terms, is the process of transforming your thoughts into the creative process that builds your life. For example: this book. It was the alchemy of an idea, transformed in mind, combined with the minds of others in the form of quotes and inspirations that came together to create something new. It wasn't magic. It was the process of using what I already had inside me. What do you have inside you today you can combine in alchemy to make magic in your life?

June 14

My intention for today is

____

____

Oops, Now What?

"When you admit you made a mistake, it frees you up to say, "Now what…?" ~ Marilyn Sherman

They say failure is simply the first attempt at success. For many, that is the end of success. They do not try again. As you practice with these daily quotes and your own stress reduction practice, where can you be a little more gentle with yourself? Where can you go back and say, "Oops!" and try again? Is there time when you scolded someone for making a mistake? Can you go back, apologize, forgive yourself, and say, "Now what?"

June 15

My intention for today is

____

____

Permission to Choose Joy

"Choose a joy you love, and you will never have to work a day in your life." ~ Anonymous

I don't believe we were put on this earth to work – to slave, toil, labor, and strife. Some might call my belief contrarian. But from it, I have built a wonderful, unique life. As I have said before, my dad taught me "Do what you love and you never work a day in your life." There are many versions of the same sentiment. I honor all the ways we choose to share our gifts, talents, and abilities with the world. If your work works for you, keep doing it. Today, I give you permission to choose joy in how you spend your days. What is one joy-filled thing you will do today?

June 16

My intention for today is

____

____

Bigger, Faster, More

"Worry about being better; bigger will take care of itself." ~ Gary Comer

One of the things I struggle with as I continue to grow, expand, and deepen my spiritual practice is the idea – our society's construct – of bigger, faster, and more. It seems that our world thrives on this. Who has the biggest hamburger? Where do you go to get the best service for your home? Which car is the fastest? Today, do not worry. Don't go for bigger. Don't go for faster. Don't go for more. Live mindfully. Live in the moment. Honor whatever size, quality, speed...and honor what is now. Life supports life, and it will take care of you.

June 17

My intention for today is

____

____

Music Soothes, Inspires, and Lives

"Music is Life..." ~ Karl Anthony

On my Everyday Mindfulness Show, I offered a series of episodes on mindful music. There are many tools to use in your mindful living practice, and music is one we often take for granted. Music is a part of the culture of the world. For some, music is a love language; they are always up on the hits and have a genre or genres they follow. For others, music is quieter and softer as the background to their lives. Today, if you have a playlist, pull it out and listen to a few songs for inspiration. If music is not a part of your practice, start by listening to a song or two. Throughout the book and on my show, you will see names of singers and songwriters with words to inspire your life.

June 18

My intention for today is

____

____

Apology Note

"I am what I am, an' I'm not ashamed."
~ Rubeus Hagrid

Is there a place in your life where you were ashamed of what you did? How you came across? What you said? It is one thing to be proud of who you are, as Hagrid from the J.K. Rowling Harry Potter series says here. It is another thing to go around strutting yourself in a way that hurts others. If I asked you in this moment to write an apology note to someone you may have hurt or wronged, how many notes would you feel called to write? It's a good mindful practice to write both apology notes and thank-you notes to people. I write one each day. I may not send all of them, but the practice of writing them helps the energy between me, my highest self, and the other person. Let the writing begin.

June 19

My intention for today is

____

____

TRUST: Total Reliance on Universal Source Today

"Trust that your wounds are exactly as the Universe planned. They were divinely placed in your life in the perfect order so that you could show up for them with love and remember the light within."
~ Gabrielle Bernstein

Do you remember your first scar? That first time you broke a bone? It's funny looking back at how as kids we are proud of these "growth moments," yet as adults we learn to be ashamed of them. We try not to let people know where we are cut, broken, or bruised. Gabrielle Bernstein invites us to look at those wounds and use them as learning moments. What is a cut, bruise, or health challenge that you have experienced? Now, as you look back, how are you better as a result of this? Keep in mind there is no big or small in healing, in wounds, or in your practice. Any experience will do.

June 20

. . . .

My intention for today is

____

____

Alphabetical Living

"Always remember that striving and struggle precede success, even in the dictionary." ~ Sarah Ban Breathnach

Did you know that each year more than 1,000 words are added to the dictionary? What did you believe about the dictionary prior to reading this statistic? I might have told you that the dictionary remained pretty much the same, encyclopedias too! Words can be your power. I often circle back and look up words to clarify meaning and proper use. Today, no matter what you are striving to create, know that you are on the way to success. If you are a little lost, find a word and look it up. You may be surprised how that may lead you over a struggle and back to your path.

June 21

My intention for today is

____

____

The Compassion Intention

"Love and compassion are necessities, not luxuries. Without them, humanity cannot survive." ~ Dalai Lama

If I could only teach one skill the rest of my days, I think it would be compassion. In our new technology-enabled world, many kids – and even some adults – have never been taught or do not know how to activate compassion. Drawing from yesterday's dictionary reading, when you look you up compassion, it means to have sympathy, concern for the suffering or misfortunes of others. How are others around you suffering? Are you paying attention? Show them compassion.

June 22

My intention for today is

____

____

What Are You Teaching?

"We teach people how to treat us." ~ Phil McGraw

There is both good news and bad news in this quote. Part of mindful living is owning your part of your life experience. Hint, hint: that means all of your experience. If you do not like how someone is treating you, you must take ownership of the experience. Life is a do-it-to-yourself project. What are you doing? Today, reflect on how you are being treated by the three people closest to you. Celebrate the relationships that work well, and work to refine those you wish could be improved. Life is the ultimate classroom.

June 23

My intention for today is

____

____

Bounce

"Success is how high you bounce when you hit the bottom." ~ George Patton

Life has its inevitable ups and downs. It's not what happens when you are down, it's how you choose to bounce. How are you bouncing? This quote was submitted by an incarcerated man; that makes it all the more special to include in our study of everyday mindfulness. He is in one of those inevitable low moments, likely even lower than yours. This man is in the process of making the most of his "home" in jail. He has a job, meals, and is finding meaning. You? What are you doing? Are you making your life a limited prison with walls, or looking up already mid-bounce?

June 24

. . . .

My intention for today is

____

____

Let Go & Become

"When I let go of what I am, I become what I might be."
~ Lao Tzu

This is not the life I thought I would have, it is the life I have chosen. One of my personal guides is Rick Finbow, a psychic medium and tarot reader. Years ago, he said to me, "Holly, you need to stop trying to be, and be." Clearly, it was an "ah ha" moment for me. When you look back in your memories, what is something someone has said to you that stopped you in your tracks, or changed the course of your trajectory? Did you act on it? Is it still relevant? No matter what the question, the answer is always evolving. What are you going to stop trying to become, and actually become in the 24-hour adventure that is today?

June 25

My intention for today is

____

____

Storytelling

"When you get right down to it, intentional living is about living your best story." ~ John C. Maxwell

You know how it goes: what you resist persists. I used to resist storytelling as childish and unnecessary. Why tell a story when I could read you the facts, data, and research on what I was telling you and why it was important? Where are you not telling your story? Or telling an incongruent story? Today, make a list. On one side, put what you believe about yourself; on the other side, look at how you are being in the world. This is intentional living. Are you living the story on the left column or the one on the right? Are they the same story? Write your own bestseller every day.

June 26

My intention for today is

____

____

Car Sickness

"Difficult roads often lead to beautiful destinations."
~ Author Unknown

The road to Hana in Hawaii is famous for being one of the curviest and hardest roads in the U.S. to navigate. It's narrow and winding with a lot of tight switchbacks and blind corners. Yet, thousands of tourists flock to drive it every month. Why? Because on the journey, you experience tropical pools, waterfalls, and beauty beyond imagine. Look at your life. What is a difficult road you have journeyed on? Was there beauty along the way? Keep going.

June 27

. . . .

My intention for today is

____

____

Plants Grow in Good Soil

"Don't go through life, grow through life."
~ Eric Butterworth

I don't have a green thumb. I often wish I did, but I was given different gifts and talents. I help people create good soil so they can grow their own life. What talents were you given (for example, writing, speaking, parenting, gardening, automotive, accounting, speaking)? How do you use those talents to create good soil to grow your life? Just like plants need new soil from time to time, you also do. Today, nourish your soil. Drink a glass of water and be present with the water. Eat a healthy meal, read a good book, balance your finances, call a friend. Don't just let life pass you by. Grow from it.

June 28

My intention for today is

____

____

Did I Miss It?

"Wherever you are, be all there." ~ Jim Elliot

On August 21, 2017, the largest lunar eclipse of all time crossed over the United States of America. A lunar eclipse is when the moon crosses in front of the sun, darkening the ground below. The first city in the U.S. to experience it was Lincoln City, Oregon. My parents happen to have a home there. So I flew out from Colorado with a guest to experience it. There were two minutes and 40 seconds of darkness suddenly at about 10 in the morning when it would normally have been full light. My guest was a photographer. When the eclipse came, he was so focused on clicking that he missed the entire event, and he didn't even get a good shot. Has this ever happened to you? You get to an event, so focused on making the event perfect, on creating a memory, that you are not fully present to it? Today, wherever you go BE ALL there or don't go. And if you ever have the chance to witness a lunar eclipse, say yes and focus on the experience.

June 29

My intention for today is

____

____

Be-YOU-2-A-Ful

"Live quietly in the moment and see the beauty of all before you. The future will take care of itself..."
~ Paramahansa Yogananda

Louise Hay made "mirror work" famous. Mirror work is the daily practice of looking at yourself in the mirror, taking a moment to connect with yourself, and stating a positive affirmation. I invite you to do that today. See your beautiful self, be quiet, and take in the beauty before you. Many of us read Facebook each day and it shows us "this day in history." You peruse the photos of where you were in years past and mindfully notice how you've changed since then. You may not bring that same awareness to the beauty you are today. As you look in the mirror, try to recognize the power of this moment. Be now. The future will take care of itself. All is well.

June 30

My intention for today is

____

____

Looking Forward & Looking Back

"The reason most people give up too fast is that they look at how far they still have to go, instead of how far they have come." ~ Anonymous

Objects in mirror may be closer than they appear. Those are the words on your car's rearview mirror. Why? Because you aren't going that way. Those images are a distant memory. The visions in the front window are where you are going. What's in your front window? Appreciate how far you have come as you pause and envision how you want this day, week, and month to look in your windshield, not your rearview mirror.

July

Freedom

Why does freedom mean so much to you? How does freedom inform your work and your personal life? What does it mean to live your freedom daily? In the month of July, we will celebrate leaders of countries, companies, families, and you. Let your freedom flag fly each day.

July 01

. . . .

My intention for today is

____

____

Desire Is Your Destiny

"I'm a success today because I had a friend who believed in me and I didn't have the heart to let him down." ~ Abraham Lincoln

I remember once my mom telling me as a child that I had very high self esteem. In the moment, I took that as a bad thing. I tried to downplay it. As I look back on my life, it is the alchemy of my own desire, coupled with other people's belief in me, that has propelled my work forward.

Look back on your own life. Who believed in you at a down moment? How can you lift someone up in the same way today?

July 02

My intention for today is

____

____

Honor it All

"Share our similarities, celebrate our differences."
~ M. Scott Peck

What if this quote was: share our differences and celebrate our similarities? How would you understand it differently? This is where I think we need to go as mindful humans that lead. No matter how you show up in the world, we need more people calling for us to share our differences and honor them, acknowledge them. Share where we are different, and how we are all different, so we can learn from one another. Then celebrate where we are similar. One of my favorite things do on social media is post photos of my family – my black sister, my gay friend, male or female, etc. I know that this is a teaching tool for someone in my community who may not be open to sharing differences as strengths and finding similarities. I'm not black, and I'm not gay. Yet I share in this different, and celebrate the strength of the One human family. Today, find someone different than you in race, thought, mind, gender, clothing...I don't care. Then find a way to celebrate the connections in your different and in your same.

July 03

My intention for today is

____

____

Celebrate Freedom!

"A holiday isn't a holiday, without plenty of freedom and fun." ~ Louisa May Alcott

No matter what flag you fly, I hope you fly it high. Fly it proud. Freedom looks different for every one of you reading this book. For some, it's choosing your clothes and your profession. For others, it's accepting what is. It's not for me to judge or define what freedom is for you and how you celebrate it. Today, I simply ask you to define your own freedom and celebrate it in your way. Never take this gift for granted.

July 04

My intention for today is

____

____

Choose Your Success

"People begin to become successful the moment they choose to be." ~ Harvey McKay

Choice...it's one of the most powerful tools we have during this human experience. We make zillions of mind-less choices each day. Those choices often come as a result of our human "programming" or beliefs, when we do not pause to consider the options and choose mindfully. We think that because we are bombarded with messaging that we can't make every choice mindful. Yet, the big ones we must. Today, look at the choices you make. Do you make them from the frame of doing what is best for you or what is best for the other person? Sometimes when you choose to put your good second, you take away from goodness in the world. Choose how to be mindful.

July 05

. . . .

My intention for today is

____

____

Affirm Life While You Live It

"Let us learn to show our friendship for a man when he is alive and not after he is dead." ~ F. Scott Fitzgerald

Mindful living doesn't mean life is great and wonderful all the time. It's how you deal with the downs, being fully present to what is. July 5 will always be a meaningful day to me. It's the birthday of a beloved friend, Nate, who passed away at age 39. If you have lived or loved at all, you most likely have at least one such memorable day when you remember a friend or family member who is no longer with us. Today, pick up a phone and tell someone how much they mean to you. I bet you surprise them. And by the law of reciprocity, I am sure they will bring you back to life and love in a new way also.

July 06

My intention for today is

____

____

Unconditional Happiness

"Happiness is only real when shared." ~ Jon Krakauer

People think I have the most glamorous job in the world as a speaker and author. Truth be told, like any other job, it has advantages and disadvantages. I've see many sites of the world solo, eaten many meals alone, and have been touched to highs of joy – only to return to a hotel room alone.

We sometimes do things by ourselves because we think, "They are too busy." "They won't have time." "I don't want to ask them because they need to be with their family or kids."

Happiness is better when shared. Do you have a moment coming up in your life when you could make a memory with someone, amp up the joy, and share?

July 07

My intention for today is

____

____

Let It Be!

"Be Feisty
Be Fearless
Be Focused
Be Fabulous
Have Fun"
~ Pegine Echevarria

July is all about freedom. We remember what a gift it is to be able to speak our truth, choose our professions, live where we want to live, and be who we came here to become. I love this inspiration by one of my teachers. Notice the word "Be." Life is not about the doing. It's not "Do feisty." We live in a feeling universe. Today, feel into being feisty, fearless, focused, and fun!

July 08

My intention for today is

____

____

Excitement Is Contagious

"When a woman rises up in glory, her energy is magnetic and her sense of possibility contagious."
~ Marianne Williamson

I start this post by confirming the same sentiment is true for men. When anyone stands up in glory, they are contagious. You are worthy and valuable. You are a magnet for good things. Who or what do you want to stand up for in glory today?

July 09

My intention for today is

____

____

Let Your Silent Voice Be Powerful

"When the whole world is silent, even one voice becomes powerful." ~ Malala Yousafzai

We live in a truly global world, pretending to be separated by walls, oceans, and borders. This wise statement by young activist Malala Yousafzai is a reminder that your voice matters at any age and in any place. What do you feel is yours to do? There is no big or small. Today, speak your truth. Maybe it's at the grocery store, a doctor's office, or in a court of law. Remember, the thoughtful use of your voice and presence makes the world a better place.

July 10

. . . .

My intention for today is

____

____

Yes to Me!

"Be yourself; everyone else is already taken."
~ Oscar Wilde

It's hard to be yourself in a world of photoshop, makeup, and push-up bras. And yes there are "enhanced" man garments also. What would it be like to be truly content with who you are? Today, mindfully take in your body, brain, and soul. Be you fully. You are here with a passion and purpose. Go about getting it done. Everyone else is already taken.

July 11

My intention for today is

____

____

Surrender to What Is

"I don't have to like it, but I do have to accept it for being exactly as it's supposed to be at this moment. Once I accept it, complaining about it becomes obsolete."
~ Rick Weaver

Do you ever have a moment when you are convinced the entire world is conspiring against you? Come on, be honest. You are human, after all. In times like these, take this tool with you. Ask yourself: "Why is this the best thing happening right now?" Then tell yourself: "This is the best thing happening right now because it is the only thing happening right now, and I believe the world is conspiring for my good." The first few times you do this, it is a head scratcher. But it's true. The world is conspiring for our good. So even when we tell ourselves "bad" things are happening, we must simply shift back and remember that, instead, this is simply what is happening right now. Therefore, it is good. Surrender.

July 12

My intention for today is

____

____

Make Up Your Mind

"Most people are about as happy as they make up their mind to be." ~ Abraham Lincoln

Each and every day, you choose who will show up in the world you are creating. What makes you happy? Are you making time in your life for those people, places, and events? Take out your calendar, and make time – time for you to be happy. Invite a friend somewhere. Think of a time in your life you have been most happy. Take yourself energetically back there.

July 13

My intention for today is

____

____

Piss-o-city A State Of Being

"The truth will set you free, but first it will piss you off."
~ Gloria Steinem

Today, I want to remind you that being a mindful person is not about being flowers and candy all the time. It's not about saying things are happy and joyful when they actually suck. Being mindful is about being where you are in the moment and doing your best to have non-judgement about it. Honor the feelings, and let them wash through you until the good returns. Yes, being sad, upset, mad, or frustrated is a thing. It's a normal thing. Accept these feelings and then choose again.

July 14

. . . .

My intention for today is

____

____

Keep Exploring

"We are, all of us, exploring a world none of us understands…searching for a more immediate, ecstatic, and penetrating mode of living…for the integrity, the courage to be whole, living in relation to one another in the full poetry of existence." ~ Hillary Rodham Clinton

Often there is a misconception, a misunderstanding, where we think, "Oh, this leader knows what he or she doing." They actually may not. The mindful leader is often the person more willing to go where nobody has gone before, even if they don't understand it. Living in these transformational times invites us to say, "I don't know. But something within me knows, and I'll make it up as I go." What do you need to make up as you go along today?

July 15

My intention for today is

____

____

Feel It Into Being

"The journey has to feel the way you want the destination to feel." ~ Danielle Laporte

There are countless books, and even passages like this one, about the power of having a goal or dream. Through visioning, I take you through the process of what attaining that goal might feel like. There is not enough talk about what Danielle Laporte mentions here. Feeling good about every step of the journey brings the desired outcome to you even faster. Today, let's take your intention you wrote at the top of this page. What does it feel like to have that as your reality today? Sit in a few moments of meditation, and feel throughout your day as if this has already happened.

July 16

My intention for today is

____

____

Balance the Giving & the Receiving

"We make a living by what we get, but we make a life by what we give." ~ Winston Churchill

Our world conditions us that it is better to give than to receive. These concepts are actually two sides of the same coin. We cannot have receiving without a giver. We cannot have a giver without a receiver. Sometimes, it is okay to take a turn as a receiver. Today, celebrate moments of life that you have received good, either expected or unexpected. Praise that. How can you receive today, allowing someone to give to you?

July 17

• •

My intention for today is

____

____

Listen More, Talk Less

"There isn't anyone you couldn't learn to love once you've heard their story." ~ Fred Rogers

Fred Rogers was an American TV icon in the late 1900s. For decades, he hosted a children's show called "Mr. Rogers' Neighborhood." On the show, Mr Rogers would introduce us to the people in his neighborhood. While it may sound a little childish, I think this is what our world needs. We need to know the people in our neighborhood. Who are they? What are they passionate about? What is their pet's name? Once you get to know someone, you learn to care. Today, look down your street? What percentage of the people do you really know? Today, get to know one more.

July 18

My intention for today is

____

____

Freedom of Choice

"The ultimate measure of a man is not where he stands in moments of comfort and convenience, but where he stands at times of challenge." ~ Darren Hardy

When I read this quote, I am reminded of the old advertisement: Life is messy, pick it up. Where are you when life gets messy? Are you running away or running to? When life is challenging for yourself or someone else, you do in fact have a choice. Will you stand with or walk away? As you continue to build your mindful practice, you build your own skill and awareness that being there for yourself or a friend or family member in need is the most valuable and precious opportunity – one that you will never be able get back. Learn to be present in times of challenge, and you will watch the challenge melt away.

July 19

....

My intention for today is

____

____

Be Where You Are

"Wherever you go, there you are!" ~ Mary Engelbreit

Where did the day go? Do you ever hear yourself asking that as you climb into bed? This is what happens when you overbook your day and run from one thing to the next, to the next, to the next. It's mindless – not mindful. Today, as you move from event to event, be sure to pause at each point along the way and fully take in the sights, sounds, smells, and feelings of the experience. When you are fully present, you invite others to slow down and do the same, making the event all the more better.

July 20

My intention for today is

____

____

Expand Your Capacity to Love

"We have within us an extraordinary capacity for love, joy and unshakable freedom." ~ Jack Kornfield

Extraordinary. Breathe in that for a minute. In a world that is constantly telling us to "fit in," Jack Kornfield invites us to be extra ordinary. Extra – that little something more. Today, take in a little more good. Give a little extra ordinary good. Open a door for someone. Buy someone's coffee. Do an errand for a neighbor. Be unshakable in your commitment to love, joy, and freedom.

July 21

My intention for today is

____

____

Accept What Is

"The first step toward change is awareness. The second step is acceptance." ~ Nathaniel Branden

Change happens. I grew up in Oregon where we would say, "If you don't like the weather, wait five minutes and it will change." And sure enough, it would. When I get a little tired or stalled in my mindfulness practice, I remember that so many of the lessons I need to know are found in nature. Today, where do you need to expand your awareness? When you know more, you do more. Where will you accept the inevitable and unavoidable change that is happening now? And that will change again. Accept what is.

July 22

My intention for today is

____

____

Resent or Forgive: Choose

"When you hold resentment toward another, you are bound to that person or condition by an emotional link that is stronger than steel. Forgiveness is the only way to dissolve that link and get free." ~ Catherine Ponder

When in your life do you believe you have been treated unfairly? How long is your list? Now put the shoe on the other foot. When have you treated others unfairly? While there are many takes on forgiveness, I don't think it's so much about the "other" person. I think forgiveness changes you. Remember, there is no other. When you resent another, you take on that resentment in you. When you forgive, you set yourself free.

July 23

My intention for today is

____

____

Keep Learning! Keep Improving!

"No matter how much experience you have, how many degrees you have, or how well known you have become — there is always something new to learn. Don't rest on your past experiences. If you do nothing to improve your skills, you won't stay where you are." ~ Laura Spencer

Life is the ultimate learning journey. At today's pace of life, every minute creates more information, experiences, and wisdom to take in. FOMO – Fear of Missing Out – is a real thing. But with this also comes countless opportunities to learn. Today, what is one thing that you can do to learn something new? Pick up an "old school" printed newspaper, buy a book you've wanted to read and commit to five pages each day, sign up for a class, or ask a question of someone. Learn something new.

July 24

My intention for today is

____

____

Flow With Universal Energy

"Adapt. Change. Or die." ~ Jeffrey Hayzlett

Jeff Hayzlett just tells it like it is. Mindful living is not about being stagnant on a meditation pillow or getting so present in a moment that time stops. Mindfulness is being so fully present in the moment that you simply you flow with it. Today, where must you adapt? What in your life needs to change? Or is there a project, behavior, or action you need to let die?

July 25

••••••••••••••••••••••

My intention for today is

____

____

Bold Freedom Expressing

"Freedom lies in being bold." ~ Robert Frost

How do you define being bold? How do express being bold? I think the fact that you are reading this book is a bold statement. Bold is not hesitating, having no fear, moving forward, breaking society's rules. We must often become bold to necessitate change. This July, we have focused on expressing our freedom mindfully and thoughtfully. That is bold. Bold is not always found in media headlines. It is equally found in quiet moments of authenticity, trust, and growth. Thank you this day for choosing to express your bold freedom in the way that serves you. Because when you serve you, you serve the world.

July 26

My intention for today is

____

____

Free To Be You & Me

"A friend is someone who gives you total freedom to be yourself." ~ Jim Morrison

I always wanted a "best friend" – a friend I could say would be with me till the end. For years and years, well into my 30s, I lamented about the thing I wished I had when I was a child – a lifelong friend. It seemed that everyone had one but me. When we get attached to a certain idea, we sometimes lose perspective and don't see things the way they are. Then I remembered my middle school times – Amanda, there was Amanda. She is still in my heart and my phone today as we joyously move toward our 50s. A friend may be someone you meet today or someone you have known since childhood. You may not talk to a true friend for years, but the moment you connect, it's like you never missed a day. Today, celebrate the friends that allow you to be yourself every day, week, month, and year of your life. Call that friend. I'm dialing Amanda now...

July 27

My intention for today is

____

____

The Ability to Respond

"Freedom is the will to be responsible to ourselves."
~ Friedrich Nietzsche

Every time I hear the word "responsible," I flip it. I say in my responsible "inside voice" that instead I have the ability to respond in this situation. That definition creates a different energy from how you normally may feel about responsibility. The weight we often associate with being responsible flips to our choice. As a person choosing calm instead of chaos through your daily applied mindfulness practice, you have the freedom to respond. You have the ability to respond. You have the choice to respond. Use applied mindfulness practices today and be responsible for your responses.

July 28

My intention for today is

____

____

Freedom in Letting Go

"One of the happiest moments in life is when you find the courage to let go of what you cannot change."
~ Unknown

Many, many...make that many...lessons of my life still have the claw marks of my fingernails as I have finally let the lessons go. Is there a place in your life where you need a reality check? Something you want to work that is not working? Yet you keep holding on, hoping it will change. Is it in your finances? Relationships? Job? Health? Do you want to be happy or right? Pick one. If you choose happy, you can find your heart, open your hands, and let go. Open to what you cannot change and make room for change that will naturally come your way. Something new and wonderful this way comes. And I know this firsthand.

July 29

My intention for today is

____

____

Free to Grieve

"Grief, I have learned, is really just love. It's all the love you want to give, but cannot. All of that unspent love gathers in the corners of your eyes, the lump in your throat, and in the hollow part of your chest. Grief is just love with no place to go." ~ Unknown

July and freedom bring up visions of fireworks, flags, summer fun, and outdoor recreation. I want to also invite you be free to grieve. Mindful living is honoring both the celebrations and the sadness. After all, it's all love. Love in different forms. If there is something coming up in your practice that makes you sad, honor that. Grief is God in action. Let it flow. Don't be ashamed, own your mindfulness. If you have mind-less grief, go there. My friends at www.beyondyourgrief.com are happy to support your tears.

July 30

. . . .

My intention for today is

____

____

Start Where You Are

"The secret of getting ahead is getting started."
~ Samuel Clemons (Mark Twain)

The first step can often be the scariest. Today, call a friend to hold your hand and take the step with you. Grab a box of Kleenex, a coffee, a glass of your favorite beverage. This now is your moment. Start where you are, and take one step. Progress is being made.

July 31

. . . .

My intention for today is

____

____

Respond or React

"Freedom is that instant between when someone tells you to do something and when you decide how to respond." ~ Jeffrey Borenstein

I am most aware of how far I have come in my mindful daily practice during those heated moments when I know the "old" me would react in a firey rage – but the the "new" me somehow operates on a deeper, more centered level. I am able to pause and consciously, thoughtfully respond. Looking back on the last few months, have you had these moments? I bet you have. Freedom is deciding how to respond. Today, keep using your new tools to cast out reaction and honor your heart-and-head responses that are now your new normal.

August

Summer Light and Experiences

Summer nights quickly give way to the fall harvest during this transition time. Our August theme is summer light and summer experiences. Take mindful moments on these long days to see, feel, sense, and know the abundance of that transition all around you and in you.

August 01

My intention for today is

____

____

Looking Up & Down

"I'm so high that the stars are below me."
~ Jim Davidson

When we were children, our neighbors Jane and Ed would take my brother and me out out every year to see the Percid meteor shower. I am guessing we were four or five years old. Memories may come and go over the years, yet feelings you never forget. Tonight, make a point to go outside and look up at the stars. This mindfulness practice will hopefully bring you a certain sense of awe and wonder that we truly are a part of something bigger than ourselves. As you look up, vision down. What do the stars see as they look at you?

August 02

My intention for today is

____

____

The Summer Stars Above

"We are not simply in the universe, we are a part of it. We are born from it. One might even say we have been empowered by the universe to figure itself out and we have only just begun." ~ Neil Degrasse Tyson

One of the most powerful mindful self-empowerment tools is the ability to ask great questions. Big questions. Deep questions. Sometimes, even totally random questions. It's not necessarily important here that you agree with Mr. Degrasse-Tyson; it's more important that you ask yourself, "Do I believe we are a part of the universe?" Enjoy where this question may take you. How does your life reflect your answer?

August 03

My intention for today is

____

____

Courage of the Heart

"Never let fear decide your fate." ~ Holly Hoffman

Fear is one of the most talked about self-help concepts. All of us spend our lives learning how to un-learn fear. Or how to use fear as our catalyst for our highest best life. Scan aspects of your life today? Where do you experience fear in the scan? Work? Home? Family? Relationships? Mindfully stop and ask yourself if you are going to let that fear block you, or open you to new possibility.

August 04

My intention for today is

____

____

Undivided Attention

"The more one does and sees and feels, the more one is able to do, and the more genuine may be one's appreciation of fundamental things like home, and love, and understanding of companionship." ~ Amelia Earhart

While we have more ways to connect and travel to distant lands now than ever before, studies report we are the most lonely generation. There is a barrier between us and the people we are trying to connect with. It may be a table, a window, a phone, or another device. Today, be mindful of where you may be lonely. Keep an eye and heart out to feel if someone else is lonely. Find a way to value true companionship. The best gift you can give is your undivided attention.

August 05

My intention for today is

____

____

Superhero In You

"One way to remember who you are is to remember who your heroes are." ~ Steve Jobs

A few years ago, a young boy named Miles was on the Make a Wish registry. He wished he could be Batman. The entire city of Gotham (a.k.a. San Francisco) stopped to make it happen. There were many actors involved in staging crime scenes and scenarios around the town. On that day, November 15, 2013, the hearts of our nation honored that superheroes are everywhere. Today, embrace your inner super power. When you identify what that is (reading, writing, speaking, crafting, etc.) go share that super power with someone else. You will unlock the key, not just to Gotham City, but to your heart.

August 06

My intention for today is

____

____

Be A Card Shark

"Fate shuffles the cards and we play."
~ Authur Schopenhauer

Playing cards is a game of science and strategy, where you have to deal with what you are dealt. No different than life. Today, what cards are in your deck? The Queen of Hearts, Nine of Diamonds, Ace of Spades? Even as I name off those cards, what stories do you tell yourself about the perception of good or bad in each? What are you telling yourself about the cards in your hands? A card shark is someone skilled at playing card games. Look at the hand that fate has shuffled for you and choose to play it skillfully.

August 07

My intention for today is

____

____

Cut The Weight

"Do not bring people in your life who weigh you down. And trust your instincts…good relationships feel good. They feel right. They don't hurt. They're not painful. That's not just with somebody you want to marry, but it's with the friends that you choose. It's with the people you surround yourselves with." ~ Michelle Obama

It's sometimes hard to like people nowadays. So much divisive-ness and mean-ness in our world. It's hard to choose compassion when people do us wrong. Mindful people are able to pause long enough to build a light-filled boundary between themselves and people who no longer serve them. "I choose to be with people who want what is best for me and I for them," says my friend Carolyn. A wise woman. Today, have enough self love to let go and let light surround you if there is someone in your life who is weighing you down.

August 08

My intention for today is

____

____

14er's Real & Metaphorical

"You don't climb mountains without a team, you don't climb mountains without being fit, you don't climb mountains without being prepared and you don't climb mountains without balancing risks and rewards. And you never climb mountains on accident – it has to be intentional." ~ Mark Udall

I live in Colorado, which is home to 53 fourteeners. That is the word for a mountain that is more than 14,000 feet high. When I first moved here, I made a life list of things to do. Climbing a fourteener was on that list. I am not an outdoorswoman, nor do I pretend to be. In August 2016, I experienced 14,000 feet for the first time. As this quote says, you don't get there accidentally. What is your real or metaphorical fourteener? That tall mountain that you desire to climb? Now every project I take on is a metaphor for the fourteener. Be intentional, get prepared, and go seek the reward of the view from the top.

August 09

My intention for today is

____

____

Feed Your Body & Soul

"Cooking with love provides food for the soul."
~ Unknown

I have a theory that fast food doesn't make us fat solely due to the calories – it's in part because it's not made with heart. I always silently bless the workers in fast food restaurants. I think we all should. Few of them have smiles on their faces. Yet, they do a job that I value. They provide food, and when I'm in a hurry, I'm not ashamed to admit I will stop in the periodic fast food restaurant.

Today, however, find or make a meal that is made with real human hands. Pause to really take in the flavors, and let it nourish your soul.

August 10

My intention for today is

____

____

Claim Your Divine Inheritance

"Every human has four endowments – self awareness, conscience, independent will, and creative imagination. These give us the ultimate human freedom. The power to choose, to respond, to change." ~ Stephen Covey

Today, I invite you to look at each of these four key concepts – self-awareness, conscience, independent will, and creative imagination. How do you define them? If you had to rate yourself on a scale of 1 to 10 on each, where would you rank? How will you use this inner knowledge to choose how you show up in the world today?

August 11

My intention for today is

____

____

Love's Barriers

"Your task is not to seek for love, but merely to seek and find the barriers within yourself that you have built against it." ~ Rumi

It's often easier to run from love than to sit in the unknown power of love. Where in your life are you running from love? This does not necessarily mean a romantic relationship. Love can be grander than that. It can show up in all areas of our life: career, money, emotions, relationships. In most cases, you may not be actually running, but you may not be allowing the energy of love in your life. If you are a "real" runner, why do you run? Are you running to something or running away from it? Your task today is to mindfully choose to be present and calm where love's presence shows up in your life.

August 12

My intention for today is

____

____

What would you do today if you were brave?

"What if we're all meant to do what we secretly dream
What would you ask if you knew you could have anything
Like the mighty oak sleeps in the heart of a seed
Are there miracles in you and me

If I were brave I'd walk the razor's edge
Where fools and dreamers dare to tread
Never lose faith, even when losing my way
What step would I take today if I were brave"
~ Jana Stanfield

In 2012, Disney released its animated movie Brave. In that movie, a sassy, redheaded princess named Merida chose to defy the custom of getting married. She chose to live a new life. A brave choice. Do you desire to do something new, or out of character for you, where you need to be brave? It may not be as big as marriage, but it could be something as bold as choosing not to eat meat. You get my point. Today in your choices, choose to be you. There is a braveness in being you, all you, all the time.

August 13

My intention for today is

____

____

Clouds & Stars

"Don't let a momentary cloud be permanent in your sky." ~ David Ault

Do you ever look to the sky and see a shape? For me, the shape I always look for is a heart. The heart is a promise from my friend Nate on the other side that he is still looking down and helping me. Not all skywriting is as deep in meaning. Some people see kites, or dinosaurs, or maybe you just see clouds. No matter what, the clouds will be moving. Today, look up and enjoy a cloud. Take in its momentary shape and beauty, and bless it as it moves. Do the same for yourself. Whatever you are going through, recognize that it, like the cloud, is temporary and is moving.

August 14

My intention for today is

____

____

Knowing & Declaring

"You were born knowing your way. Your task is not to learn but to remember." ~ Chuck Gallaher

I use the word knowing all the time. For me this word is a deep, deep felt sense in me that I know. I know 100 percent that something is happening, did happen, or will happen. Using my affirmative statements, I declare it into being. Today, use the power of your word. What do you know for sure? Your words are your seeds. Plant them. Speak them. Declare them into being.

August 15

My intention for today is

____

____

National Day of Relaxation

"Every now and then go away, have a little relaxation, for when you come back to your work your judgment will be surer. Go some distance away because then the work appears smaller and more of it can be taken in at a glance and a lack of harmony and proportion is more readily seen." ~ Leonardo da Vinci

In a world that bleeds stress and anxiety, today be a rebel. You've been exploring everyday mindfulness now for a while. Relaxation is the state of distancing yourself and being free from tension and anxiety. While I invite you to take this whole day, if you can't take that much time, just practice for five to 15 minutes to simply relax, breathe, and feel harmony. May every day invite you to find moments of relaxation that result in more productivity, peace, and prosperity.

August 16

My intention for today is

____

____

Sunrise & Sunset

"A dawn always promises a new beginning,
Whereas...
A sunset always promises a beautiful ending."
~ Anthony T. Hincks

No matter what, I know for sure that the sun will rise tomorrow and the sun will set tonight. In both of those things, I find good. Today, what do you know for sure? Enjoy the truth found in the light.

August 17

My intention for today is

____

____

Recalculating

"...there are no wrong turns, only unexpected paths."
~ Mark Nepo

If we have learned nothing else in our lives, we have learned to expect the unexpected. I would go so far as to advise you to expect the unexpected...and celebrate it. If you live a life on a schedule – get up at 7, at work by 9, off at 5, drive the same route home – today I'm going to challenge you to intentionally recalculate that. There is a mindfulness about waking up to a set routine – and changing it. Often, we can find a sacred opening that allows someone or something to show up. Today, recalculate your day and celebrate the unexpected path. You will build your life muscles for when the next totally unexpected thing comes your way.

August 18

My intention for today is

____

____

Vulnerable Openness

"This day my heart is open, my arms outstretched in trusting and receiving the presence of Love."
~ Dr. Patty Luckenbach

Do what this quote says. Open your arms wide, outstretch them. Does it feel a little funny? It can feel a bit strange to do this with your body. Most of us keep our arms down or near our sides. This time, keep your arms open. Breathe. Receive. Breathe. Receive. Now with your mind energy, feel love, joy, peace, or harmony coming toward your torso. If you initially feel a little concern, stay with that until it dissolves and the light of your vulnerability becomes comfort. Take that newfound comfort in love with you today.

August 19

My intention for today is

____

____

Complain: Join The Chorus

"Sing to your favorite childhood song, Christmas carol or make a rap." ~ Scott Friedman

It's human nature to default to wanting to complain. Our chaotic world feeds the complaining all around you. As a mindful leader, you do not have to choose or condone this behavior in your life. Today, when someone comes to complain to you or you find yourself complaining, try singing it out loud. I bet the complaint becomes a little funnier and a lot less important.

August 20

My intention for today is

____

____

Pre-Season Football

"The most valuable player is the person who makes the most players valuable!" ~ Peyton Manning

Summer is ending – are you ready for some football? I find football is one of those areas where you are either in or you are out. There are not a lot of people who are on the sidelines about football. Because of that, a lot of family feuds happen over football. Peyton Manning has a great take on it. Today, look around you. Who is on your team? Who is your MVP? Who can you empower to be a better player? Go thank them today.

August 21

My intention for today is

____

____

Acknowledge the In-between

"Be humble for you are made of the Earth. Be noble for you are made of the stars." ~ Serbian proverb

Some quotes simply stand alone. This one, submitted by a mindful friend, is one of them. What does this quote mean to you? How will you live in the place of balance between the Earth and the stars today?

August 22

My intention for today is

____

____

Purposeful Determination

"I think I benefited from being equal parts ambitious and curious. And of the two, curiosity has served me best."
~ Michael J Fox

Living a chaos-free life is not always the easy choice in our world – especially when our world today seems to choose so much chaos. You have to strengthen your ambition and curiosity almost every day. When times get tough and I am challenged, I often have to choose fight or flight. Or I can choose whether or not to be curious. You have the same choices. My advice is to choose curious. I wonder where this conversation, choice, or path is taking me? Today, when the world is coming at you full force, choose curiosity and stay determined not to get down in the chaos.

August 23

My intention for today is

____

____

Laughter Yoga

"Once you laugh at something, it ceases to have power over you." ~ Sonia Choquette

At times in serious business meetings, I have to back my brain out of the group and see myself in the meeting room and all the people around the table. From this "fly over" vantage point, you almost have to laugh. What is so serious? What is going on here? Few things in life are truly life threatening. Every once in a while, step out of a serious situation, look across it, and give yourself permission to laugh. A few years ago, laughter yoga became a thing. People were actually teaching people how to laugh again. When was the last time you truly laughed? Life is too mysterious to take too seriously. Today, I invite you to laugh. Heck, invite others to laugh with you. Take back your power.

August 24

My intention for today is

____

____

Flowers In The City

"When you take a flower in your hand and really look at it, it's your world for the moment. I want to give that world to someone else. Most people in the city rush around, so they have no time to look at a flower. I want them to see it whether they want to or not."
~ Georgia O'Keeffe

Our August theme is summertime life. Summer brings flowers and grass, gardens and trees. When did you last let your feet touch the Earth? I mean really touching the Earth – taking your shoes off and putting your feet in the soil. Many of us live in cement cages. Today, as part of reducing your stress, go touch the Earth, commune with a flower, hug a tree. Wisdom and simplicity can be found all around us when you stop to look. What can nature teach you this day?

August 25

My intention for today is

____

____

Memories Are Best When Shared With A Friend

"If you have nothing in life but a good friend, you're rich." ~ Michelle Kwan

A few years back, my mom's best friend, Cinda, passed away. That same year, I moved away, leaving many of my friends. One night, my mom and I cried our eyes out on the phone missing the companionship of friendship. Knowing there is one person out there that knows your secrets, and likes you anyway, is wealth beyond a checkbook. One person that you have made just one fond memory with brings richness. Meaningful friendship for many is a lost art today, one that all but disappeared with the rotary phone. Today, take a moment to share a memory with an old friend or make a new memory with a new friend. With this, you are already wealthy.

August 26

My intention for today is

____

____

Funniness & Forgiveness

"Always forgive your enemies — nothing annoys them so much." ~ Oscar Wilde

Why is one of the most important things we can do – forgive – often our last resort? Where in your life is it time to forgive? Remember, forgiveness is never about the other person; it's about us freeing ourselves from the impact we choose to allow another person to have on us. Today, I hope this quote makes you smile, and maybe even laugh. I've won many an argument simply by my ability to walk in a room with someone who has "done me wrong" and be the bigger person. I am not willing to be your enemy. As a result, you grow and I go mindfully forward in joy.

August 27

My intention for today is

____

____

Summer Camp Barges

"A ship in port is safe, but that's not what ships are built for." ~ Grace Hopper

Did you ever go to summer camp as a kid? I did. On the last night of our camp, all the campers would get together and build barges, little floating rafts. Each cabin would build one. On each raft there was a candle. The barge was then released in a little lake signifying the end of camp and that our light would go forward in the world. Campers would sing a song that went something like this: "Barges, I would like to go with you; I would like to sail the ocean blue." Where do you need to set your ship or barge to sail today? How can you keep that childlike light growing this day and send it forth into the world?

August 28

My intention for today is

____

____

All Systems Go

"Say "yes" to life and see how life suddenly starts working for you rather than against you." ~ Eckhart Tolle

When NASA launches a space shuttle, the commander will say, "All Systems Go!" just before launch and once all the checks and balances have been made. It's already the end of August. You've been checking and balancing. You've been practicing your intentions, visions, gratitude, beliefs, and more. All systems are go. Say yes to life and let the world work for you.

August 29

My intention for today is

____

____

Unconditional Friendship

"A friend is one that knows you as you are, understands where you have been, accepts what you have become, and still, gently allows you to grow."
~ William Shakespeare

Life is the process of continuous growth. They say you are the aggregate of the friends you surround yourself with. An unconditional friend is one who loves you no matter what and no matter how you change. Do your friends invite you to grow, or stay the same? Choose carefully. How do you invite your friends to grow with you?

August 30

My intention for today is

____

____

National Grief Awareness Day

"Just as the sun comes up every morning, surely I will move through this grief and beyond."
~ Georgena Eggleston

Mindful living often requires thoughtful conversations. Grief and grieving are natural parts of life and you need to move through them. Today, who do you grieve that may no longer be in your life? This may be a friend or family member who is still alive or someone who has passed. Honor your grief, and celebrate how this person lives on in your life. When you honor grief, you honor life.

August 31

My intention for today is

____

____

Risk What You've Dreamed

"You cannot get what you've never had unless you're willing to do what you've never done." ~ Anonymous

Some people have a bucket list – a list of things they want to do before they die. I prefer to talk about a "life list." What are the things on your list that you wish you could do in life? If your life ended today, what would you regret not doing? Get going. There are no big or small items on a "life list." They are all important. Stare fear and hesitation in the eye, and go forward.

September

Spirituality

September for so many is back to school from the lazy days of summer. September is often full of birthdays and new beginnings. This month's gathering of quotes is designed to educate you on spiritual concepts and words inspired by some of my most favorite authors.

September 01

My intention for today is

____

____

Labor of Love

"Consider how hard it is to change yourself and you'll understand what little chance you have in trying to change others." ~ Unknown

Early September in the United States means Labor Day. In theory, it is a day for the laborers to have a day off, a holiday. Now, it is more of a retail sales holiday. The official end of summer. Today, look at the people in your life. Are some of them "a lot of work"? Do you labor hard to keep them in your life? Maybe this is the time you thank them for coming into your life and bless them on their way.

September 02

My intention for today is

____

____

Time

"They say time changes things, but you have to actually change them yourself." ~ Andy Warhol

Change is inevitable, but how you change is a choice. Each fall, our surroundings change as leaves fall and rains come. Where do you most desire change in your life? Is it health, finances, relationships? Now is a great time to take a class, read a book, engage in a new conversation. Make time for change.

September 03

My intention for today is

____

____

Courage of the Heart

Periodically, I invite you to go back to the definitions of key words, to really look at the word and what it means. In our 24/7 world, we often misuse words. Today's word is courage.

cour·age

the ability to do something that frightens one
strength in the face of pain or grief

Courage for me is defined as living from the core of your heart. How will you live from the core of what your heart is telling you to become today? Today, become something that frightens you. Note: I wrote become, not do. What will you become this day? Fun? Easeful? Joyful? Wealthy? Healthy? Centered? Aware? Awake?

September 04

My intention for today is

____

____

God's Business Is Good Business

"If you wish to know the truth about your business or your profession, know that it is an activity of good. It is an activity of your partnership with the infinite."
~ Ernest Holmes

One way to reduce stress in your work life is to remember that your work is the way you circulate your good in the world. Today, align your work, trusting and knowing it is good. See good on both sides of the table, and watch how more good comes your way.

September 05

My intention for today is

____

____

See the Good

"The situation may not always be the best, but you can be the one to bring out the best in the situation."
~ Jake French

Our inspirational quote today comes from motivational speaker and my friend...no, my adopted brother...Jake French. Jake experienced a tragic accident at a young age that left him in a wheelchair. He, like all of us, had a choice to be bound to the chair or to get moving. Each day, Jake French inspires with his choice to bring out the good. Today, look at the aspect of your life that you label as "bad" and find a way to bring in some good.

September 06

My intention for today is

____

____

People Are Watching What You Are Teaching

"Being a role model is the most powerful form of educating." ~ John Wooden

We all have the opportunity and responsibility to be role models for one another. In the classroom of life, it is the most effective way to teach. What are you teaching the world today by your actions? Share your mindfulness practice with a friend today. Educate them on how everyday, a few moments of mindfulness can change their world.

September 07

My intention for today is

____

____

Reverse Mentoring

"You are never too young to lead, and we are never too old to learn." ~ Kofi Annan

It used to be accepted as truth that only older, wiser people were our teachers. One of the most exciting things about how our world is changing is that we can do away with that rule and create a new rule. Today, the youth are teaching and mentoring the wisdom keepers, and vice versa. This circulation of experience, wisdom, and knowledge makes for a smarter world. Who will you mentor or ask to mentor you on this day?

September 08

My intention for today is

____

____

Revise Your Dictionary

"Definitions belong to the defiers, not the defined."
~ Toni Morrison

I found myself at a library recently looking around and thinking about things you no longer find there. A card catalog or a set of encyclopedias may be on that list. We have common definitions of words; yet each day, new words get added to the dictionary. Often as I write, I have to go back to the dictionary to make sure I am using the right word, in the correct way. Then I get to choose if I accept that definition. Today, as you apply your mindfulness practice, if you find yourself in a disagreement, go back to the words you use and make sure you are using them correctly – or have the same definition as the one with whom you disagree.

September 09

My intention for today is

____

____

Walking Walden Pond

"Go confidently in the direction of your dreams and live the life you have imagined." ~ Henry David Thoreau

My car is my driving place of discovery. Once in a while, I look out and read a sign that tells me, "Go this way." That happened on a trip outside of Boston. Suddenly, the sign read "Walden Pond." I parked, ran down to see, and discovered I was at the location that made Henry David Thoreau famous. I had, in fact, gone confidently and followed the signs in a direction I had not anticipated, and found a new experience of imagination. How will you veer off the trail today to find the life you have imagined?

September 10

My intention for today is

____

____

Intentional Technology Usage In the Present Moment

Technology and social media are not inherently bad or good. It's how you use them that makes them so. Be mindful of what intention you have and what outcome you want before you post, comment or use a new technology. If you can't think of a good one of each of those, you may be better served skipping it altogether."
~ Phil Gerbyshak

You start off your time in this book each day with a place to set your intention. Intention setting helps you focus your energy in motion. Intention setting actually aligns your energy with Universal energy to gain the outcome you desire. It's easy to lose our mindfulness practice in the mindless world of social media. Today, set an intention for your use of social media. Place that word or phrase where you do most of your social posting, and be mindful that your posts matter.

September 11

My intention for today is

____

____

9/11 Never Forget

"If we learn nothing else from this tragedy, we learn that life is short and there is no time for hate."
~ Sandy Dahl, wife of Flight 93 pilot Jason Dahl

Tragic days, like 9/11, transform our world forever. We remember them as a collective and feel them in our individual hearts. Today, my invitation is to look inside yourself and be honest in asking: Is there hate in your heart somewhere? That little seed can so easily become a bigger thing. The first way to never forget is to release any hate in your heart.

September 12

My intention for today is

____

____

National Mindfulness Day

"Mindfulness isn't difficult, we just need to remember to do it." ~ Sharon Salzberg

Today is National Mindfulness Day. Have deep respect and gratitude for your investment in this book and your mindfulness practice. Deepen your practice this day by adding a few extra minutes, adding something new to your practice, or simply reflecting on how your practice is making you your highest and best self.

September 13

....

My intention for today is

____

____

We Are All Laborers, Craftsmen, and Artists

"He who works with his hands is a laborer.
He who works with his hands and his head a craftsman.
He who works with his hands, and his head, and his heart is an artist."
~ Saint Francis of Assisit

Titles limit our mindful living in so many ways. Often, we accidentally put a high paying job on a pedestal and a lower paying job on a low rung of the ladder. As a part of your inspiring practice today, consciously remove those false labels and remember that we all support each other in living the best life. Today, love the construction work, doctor, lawyer, teacher and mother/father – for all our jobs matter.

September 14

My intention for today is

____

____

Conscious Agreements

"The space for what you want in your life, is already being filled with what you are willing to settle for."
~ Carolyn Strauss

Life is a do-it-to-yourself project. So what are you doing to yourself? Are you reaching for that dream or settling for what is? There is no right or wrong – only your perception of it. Today, raise the bar, stop settling. What new experience is just within your reach?

September 15

My intention for today is

____

____

I Can't! Or, I Choose Not To

"You can't coach the uncommitted." ~ Waldo Waldman

All of us have trigger words – words that, when we hear them, trigger us to feel. Some of those words for me are "I can't," with very few exceptions. Can't is simply the choice not to. Where are you saying you can't, maybe I can't afford it, or I don't have the time? This is rarely actually true. Where are you choosing not to? What's left? Where is that one commitment you still have not made to yourself? Make it today. You can't coach or change what you are not committed to.

September 16

My intention for today is

____

____

Three-Ring Circus

"It's the GREATEST show on Earth. Not the adequate show on Earth." ~ Kevin Burke

Growing up, it was "cool" to go to the circus. My, how times have changed! Now, it's not only not cool, it's very unpopular. Some would even call it cruel. Barnum and Bailey, in its heyday, created what was known as The Greatest Show on Earth. It had incredible lights, showmanship and spectacle, visions of things you'd see nowhere else. It provided feelings and memories that could only be created at the circus. While a circus may not be a "thing" anymore, the feelings produced by lights, spectacle, and memories can still be had. What act would you create in your circus? Lions, Tigers, and Bears, oh my! How can you make it – your life – the GREATEST show on Earth today?

September 17

My intention for today is

____

____

Happy Becoming Day!

"The whole point of being alive is to evolve into the complete person you were intended to be."
~ Oprah Winfrey

I have visions of a day when not only do we celebrate our birthday, but we celebrate our becoming day. Because while our birth is amazing, the journey of what we become each day after that birth-day is truly a miracle. Who do you desire to become? This may not have anything to do with your profession; it may mean an energy, an experience, a passion, or a hobby. Today, September 17, is my birthday. I invite you to the party of your becoming. Celebrate your path with me this day.

September 18

My intention for today is

____

____

Consistent Success

"Success doesn't come from what you do occasionally, it comes from what you do consistently." ~ Marie Forleo

I have a note on my desk that reads "progress is being made." We all have a daily "to do" list. Pay the bills, shower, go to work, keep the house clean. No matter what is on it, it seems the list keeps circulating – one day it may be long, one day short. Today, activate a little consistency and watch your progress being made.

September 19

My intention for today is

____

____

Work – A Four-Letter Word

"I didn't get there by wishing for it or hoping for it, but by working for it." ~ Estée Lauder

One of the most important things my dad taught me was: do what you love and you never work a day in your life. Since that day, work for me has always been a "bad word" or a four-letter word. While there have been many careers for me, from retail sales to banking to baseball to meeting planning, I have always kept this question at the heart of every employment decision: "Could I love this work?" Today, make a list of what you love about the work you get to do. Discover gratitude for it.

September 20

My intention for today is

____

____

Rules Were Meant to Be Broken

"If you obey all the rules, you miss all the fun."
~ Katharine Hepburn

It has been said that all you need to know you learned in kindergarten. What if that were simply untrue? While growing up, and maybe even still today, I have often been known as the "good girl." But I'll tell ya, the times I have been the "wild woman" have been more fun. Rules were meant to be learned, understood, and sometimes bent...just a little. Today, mindfully bend a rule and see how your life may grow just a little.

September 21

My intention for today is

____

____

International Peace Day

"It is not enough to talk about peace, one must believe in it. And it is not enough to believe in it, one must work for it." ~ Eleanor Roosevelt

Every Sunday at the end of our church service, the congregation holds hands to sing the song, "Let there be peace on Earth and let it begin with me." Perhaps you do something similar in your church, too. Some Sundays, I sing the song and feel peace in my life. Other weeks, I sing it and struggle with, "Am I really feeling peace this week?" Today is International Peace Day. Think of a place you may be less peaceful than you desire and find a way to work toward peace. Peace in your home and your life brings a little more peace to the world.

September 22

My intention for today is

____

____

A Whole New World: I Dare You To Close Your Eyes

"Imagination is the true magic carpet."
~ Norman Vincent Peale

In the movie Aladdin, the prince and the princess ride around on a magic carpet. The movie's theme song says "Don't you dare close your eyes." Because I am a romantic at heart, a few years back I tried to create a magic carpet business trip. I closed my eyes and offered up an affirmation that the trip would be as easy as a magic carpet ride. Well, my trip was far from magical. My wallet was stolen, flights were delayed, the food was awful. I swore I would never imagine a magic carpet ride trip again. After I recounted the story to a friend, she corrected me, "Holly, the true purpose of your trip was that no matter what the obstacle, you can be lifted above it. That is the real magic carpet ride." Today, activate your curiosity and wonder to rise above on your magic carpet, no matter what obstacle is in your way. Dream! And don't dare close your eyes.

September 23

My intention for today is

____

____

Intentionally Focus

"Mindful performance is about taking strategic action, backed by wisdom and intentionality, so you can focus on what truly matters." ~ Angela Buttimer

Use your practice and this quote today to bring together your head action, heart wisdom, and intentional alignment to manifest what matters to you. In the stillness of this moment, ask yourself:

- What action can I take today to remain focused?
- Where can I activate the wisdom of my soul?
- How can I intentionally activate my mindfulness in daily life?

September 24

My intention for today is

____

____

Mindfulness & Music

"People who show you new music are important."
~ Unknown

I find that music speaks when words are lacking. From time to time, a client or friend will introduce me to a new song that moves them. Music opens a window to the world within them that they may not be able to put into words. I find this is especially true with men. Today, find a song or piece of music that lights your heart on fire. Share it with a friend.

September 25

My intention for today is

____

____

Park Your Car, Pave A New Trail

"If you don't like the road you're walking, start paving another one." ~ Dolly Parton

In 2013, having never lived anywhere else, I packed up my life in Oregon and moved to Denver, Colorado. The life I was living was working, but it was time for a new start. While the road didn't always look the way I thought it would, the new path introduced me to new parts of my heart I would not have otherwise experienced if I had stayed in the safe known world of Oregon. Where are you staying safe, driving the same roads, walking the same paths, and eating the same foods? Today, if you don't like the road or trail you are on, park, pause, stop. Decide if it's time to pave a new one.

September 26

My intention for today is

____

____

Spark a Love of Learning

"Once a child learns to use a library, the doors of learning are always open." ~ Laura Bush

Our September theme has been all about schools, technology, and learning. For many generations, learning began at a library. As technology has changed the nature of our world, some suspected that libraries would lose their relevance. That is not the case. Libraries today are busier now than ever before. People are connecting in classes, reading groups, via the internet, and in quiet reading time. What can you do to spark your love of learning?

September 27

My intention for today is

____

____

Circulate Knowledge

"If you get, give. If you learn, teach." ~ Maya Angelou

I think our school system is a little interesting. From the day you are old enough to enter school, you are taught to know all the answers. Then one day you graduate, and suddenly you are thrust into a world where being a "know-it-all" is frowned upon. Your life pretty quickly becomes about knowing not all the right answers, but all the right questions. As Maya Angelou says, true power is knowing how to circulate your good in such a way that what you know – whether answers or questions – you share. In that circulation, we build a better world. What do you know today that you can share?

September 28

....

My intention for today is

____

____

T.A.G – Talented And Gifted

"There needs to be a lot more emphasis on what a child can do instead of what he cannot do."
~ Dr. Temple Grandin

When I was growing up, our school system had a program called TAG, or Talented and Gifted. Very early on in my education, I learned I was not in the TAG program. I grew up thinking I was with the not so talented and gifted. Yet, we are all talented and gifted in our own way. Today, make a list of your talents and gifts. How will you choose to share those with the world? Tag, you're it!

September 29

My intention for today is

____

____

Open Doors, Open Possibilities

"Sometimes we stare so long at a door that is closing that we see too late the one that is open."
~ Alexander Graham Bell

Where in your life is a door closing? Where is a door closing you do not want to admit is closing? Life is like an accordion – it opens and it closes. We breathe in new air and breathe out old. Today, look around for the open door. Be willing to walk in that direction. Bless the closing door, thank it for what you have learned, and keep walking.

September 30

My intention for today is

____

____

Permission Slip To Change

"I give myself permission to be all I can be...To be passionate and free." ~ Karen Drucker

We all used to roll our eyes at field trip time, knowing we all had to have mom's or dad's permission to go on the trip. Funny how those little memories and rules still inform our life today. Where in your life are you waiting for someone's permission to change? Permission Granted!

October

Harvest of Spirits

As our year fades to winter, these quotes are here to inspire you to stay the course on your daily intentions, goals, dreams, and plans. Everyday mindfulness: keep returning to your calm.

October 01

My intention for today is

____

____

National Journal Writing Day

"Everyone has a book within them. Everyone has to write it thinking, 'How will I help other people? What will the book do to touch lives?'" ~ Joachim de Posada

As I said in yesterday's post, I never had a dream to become an author. What I found as I put words on the page was that a book wanted to be written by me. For some of you, it may not be a book. Maybe it's an article, a blog, a sentence, a paragraph. No matter how you perceive it, big or small, today let your wisdom flow on the pages of your life. Ask your intuition who needs to read it, and then share. Your words and wisdom, even if never shared with anyone but you, will touch your life. Who knows – maybe your life is the only one that needs what you have to write. That may be enough. Get it on the page.

October 02

My intention for today is

____

____

Open To Feel The Feelings

"In this moment, I can find misery or meaning, boredom or motivation. I can expand the hatred in the world, or I can amplify love. In all the chaos, I can find stillness and joy within." ~ Brendon Burchard

Our world is struggling to find calm in the chaos because we unfortunately often turn off the mind and the heart. By reading this book, writing your daily intentions, and exploring how to apply mindful practices to your life, you set a higher example. Thank you for expanding, amplifying, and being still and joyful. Open to your feelings, expand your words, and experience enlightenment for all the world to see.

October 03

My intention for today is

____

____

Release What's Not Working

"Every situation in life is temporary. So when life is good, make sure you enjoy and receive it fully. And when life is not so good, remember that it will not last forever and better days are on the way." ~ Jenni Young

How often at the end of a day, week or month, do we ask ourselves, "Where did the day go? Where did the week go? Where did the month go?" Today, center in and remember the power of the experience you are having in this moment. Celebrate it and feel the new feelings already on the way to you.

October 04

My intention for today is

____

____

Create Your Altar

"Your sacred space is where you can find yourself over and over again." ~ Joseph Campbell

One of my favorite places in my home is my altar. Perhaps you have one? If not, that is okay, too. An altar is simply a space in your home where you keep items, momentos of things that have meaning for you. I used to think an altar had to be a big thing, a traditional sacred space. What I have learned over time is that altars are everywhere. They are the shelves where we post family photos, a wall of quotes, or sentimental items. Maybe your purse is sacred to you. If you don't yet have a "sacred space" of your own, take a few moments today to create one. If you do, go visit it and feel the joy of the items you have on your altar. Pay attention to how they bring you back to the mindfulness of what matters.

October 05

My intention for today is

____

____

Recovering Perfectionist

"The universe doesn't allow perfection."
~ Steven Hawking

As you look around, do you see all the flaws in life, or do you see only perfection? Today, give yourself permission to see the perfection in the imperfection. In what way is your imperfection a gift to the world?

October 06

• •

My intention for today is

____

____

Chin up!

"Keep your face to the sun and you will never see the shadows." ~ Helen Keller

Without the darkness, we can never truly appreciate the light. October in the Northern hemisphere is that time when the days begin to grow shorter. It's easy to mourn the passing of the light. But if you look really closely during the darkness, you see the stars. As you navigate today, when a challenge comes your way, look for the light. As funny as this may sound, simply look up to the ceiling light in your office, a lampshade on a table, a stoplight if driving. Keep your chin up and look around you, for light is everywhere.

October 07

My intention for today is

____

____

Trust You Are Always Supported

"I live in the faith that there is a Presence and Power greater than I am that nurtures and supports me in ways I could not even imagine. I know that this Presence is All knowing and All power and is Always right where I am."
~ Ernest Holmes

You have likely been practicing with this book and these concepts for several months. Even if they were once foreign to you, now they are becoming more comfortable. Today, breathe in and look around. Smile at all you have created. That is the presence and power of good. This good is always where you are and always expanding. Whatever you need today – a client, an answer, a diagnosis, a friend – ask for it. Trust it is appearing at the right time.

October 08

My intention for today is

____

____

Reborn Each Day

"Each night, when I go to sleep, I die. And the next morning when I wake up, I am reborn."
~ Mahatma Gandhi

There are times when we interpret words or phrases from the place where we are. For example "born again" for some has a religious meaning, like "born-again Christian." It that works for you, great. If it doesn't, great. I have no judgement. What I do know is my cells rejuvenate – are born again – over and over in my lifetime. My money rejuvenates, my relationships. Re-born is simply to bring back to life. To complete a change. Where are you "reborn" or "rebirthing" yourself with your stress reduction and mindful inspirations? Celebrate how you are new, for you, through your practice.

October 09

My intention for today is

____

____

The One & Only

"Don't be a, be THE." ~ Ryan Avery

Mindful living and leadership come from the daily practice of being fully present in the moment. Owning who you are, and who you are not. Ryan Avery made a commitment to be the best Ryan Avery on the planet. Anyone can be "a," it takes something special to become "the." Where is the place in life you are called to be "the" best? Go after that today.

October 10

My intention for today is

____

____

Manifesting Normacles

"Miracles are a constant; they are the norm. Maybe we should really call them "Normal-cles."
~ Michelle Medrano

Did you know there are over 37 trillion cells in your human body? That is 37 trillion miracles you are experiencing in this very moment. To be alive is a miracle. As you go about your day, look around. Driving a car is a miracle...having a roof over your head, a miracle. Celebrate the miracles all around you.

October 11

My intention for today is

____

____

Receive With Ease

"Prepare your mind to receive the best that life has to offer." ~ Ernest Holmes

As you continue to develop your everyday mindfulness practice, there may be moments when you find you have your foot on the gas pedal of life. You are driving straight forward to the dreams you always dreamed. Then something happens. You realize a big dream. Like one you never thought possible. Then out comes the brake. You find you have your foot on the gas and the brakes at the same time. The world can only do for you what it can do through you. Today, feel yourself taking your foot off the gas and off the brakes, and allow yourself to simply receive.

October 12

My intention for today is

____

____

Look For The Open Door

"I was smart enough to go through any door that opened." ~ Joan Rivers

Are you a knocker – a person who, when you visit someone, knocks before entering? Or do you just try the door and walk in? It's a curious question to ask. When do you feel the need to knock and wait, and when do you feel comfortable to just walk in? Now you can take this literal scenario and make it a figurative one. Where in your life are you knocking – waiting for a door to open – versus simply just walking on through? You are worthy, you are guided. What door do you want to walk on through? See it opening, keep walking today.

October 13

My intention for today is

____

____

Accept Now

"Whatever the present moment contains, accept it as if you had chosen it." ~ Eckhart Tolle

Do you ever wonder if you are having the right experience? Like, things are so challenging that you think you must have done something wrong? That is your "humanness" talking. How do you know you are having the right experience? Because it is the experience you are having. Today, let go of any sense of right and wrong, and accept where you are without judgement. Whether you chose it, or it chose you, say "yes" and keep moving.

October 14

My intention for today is

____

____

Sometimes You Just Know

"Knowing what must be done does away with fear."
~ Rosa Parks

Oprah Winfrey has a section in her magazine titled "What I Know For Sure." Over the years, she has shared anecdotes on life and living – things she has experienced through the wisdom of life. Sometimes, you just know. Call it gut instinct. Call it intuition. I call it knowing. When you reach that level of truth and trust, you act almost instinctively without thinking. Today, ask your inner voice what it wants you to know. Act upon what you hear.

October 15

My intention for today is

____

____

Sailing & Flowing

"I am not afraid of storms for I am learning how to sail my ship." ~ Louisa May Alcott

The original definition of telemetry is the process of gathering data to measure remote destinations using radio signals. A telemeter is the instrument that is used for the measurements – the "remote measures." Sometimes, this is how we have to look in order to move our lives – from a place of "remote measure." Today, step back from doing, and pause and let yourself be. As you look upon where you are in life, stepping back remotely, don't be afraid gather data, measure data, and feel data. With what you know, how do you choose to continue the course? The most important thing is to keep sailing.

October 16

My intention for today is

____

____

Ask for Feedback

"Sometimes you can't see yourself clearly until you see yourself through the eyes of others." ~ Ellen Degeneres

Our best learning tends to happens in relationship. That provides the good and the interesting. It can be a valuable exercise to ask people around us for feedback on how they perceive us – not so much to see that they are right or wrong, but to check our own perceptions of how we show up in the world. I often say to myself, "I'm not a girly girl." When I checked that perception with several men and women friends, they all laughed saying, "Holly, you are one of the most womanly women we know." Today, ask for feedback. Discover and choose how you want to show up in the world.

October 17

My intention for today is

____

____

Withholding Love

"You never lose by loving. You always lose by holding back." ~ Barbara De Angelis

Our world is always focused on giving love. Mindfulness practitioners (that's you – a person trying to be more mindful) often realize one of the greatest challenges is not in giving love, it's in letting love in. Today, look around you, feel around you. Where are you not truly recognizing where love is coming in to you? For example, love may come from a smile, a check, a hug, or phone call. When you pause to really experience love coming your way in all its forms, you open up more ways for love to be in your life.

October 18

My intention for today is

____

____

You Matter!

"The art of acting morally is behaving as if everything we do matters." ~ Gloria Steinem

Suicide rates in this country are rising to tragic levels. Often underneath this epidemic is a story of someone telling him or herself that they don't matter. That their presence in the world does not make a difference. In the 24/7 rush of life, it's critical for all of us to pause and remember that we matter. Today, make a list of five ways you personally matter in the world. You can't make a wrong list. You matter because you take the kids to school or you work a great job or you tend a garden or cook a meal. Everyone and everything matters. Now that you have reminded yourself, go remind someone else today how they matter.

October 19

My intention for today is

____

____

Please Take Me Off Your Pedestal

"I feel like the peer of whoever it is that I'm talking to."
~ Unknown

It's easy in life to put someone on a pedestal, or even to put yourself on one. I will never forget attending an event where I got seated next to the keynote speaker. He and I, of course, were chatting back and forth rather casually. Eventually, I said to him, "You know you are a big shot." And he gently, kindly asked me to remove him from the pedestal I had placed him on. He reminded me that we are all just people. Who do you need to take off a pedestal today?

October 20

My intention for today is

____

____

Bylaws, Policies & Procedures

"There are no rules here – we are trying to accomplish something." ~ Thomas Edison

In my first book Ctrl + Alt + Believe: Reboot Your Association For Success, I have a whole section on knowing the rules. Here's why: because those who know the rules, know how to break them. In life, I never considered myself a rule breaker. Then I came to realize that the best, most successful people were often the ones breaking all the rules. What do you want to accomplish in your life today? Find a rule and then go one step to the left or right of the "rule." You just may open yourself up to accomplish something you once thought impossible.

October 21

My intention for today is

____

____

Excuses Do Not Excuse You

"If you're serious about changing your life, you'll find a way. If you're not, you'll find an excuse." ~ Jen Sincero

I hope this has never happened to you, but I bet it has. There has been a moment in your life when you settled for something you knew was not a fit, maybe a job or a relationship. You bent yourself into a pretzel to make it fit. There was a time in my life I settled for a retail job because I simply couldn't wrap my brain around becoming a highly-paid inspirational speaker/coach. I had every excuse in the book. Today, what's your excuse. Are you ready to take a chance? Re-write your script. Your excuse will not excuse your greatness.

October 22

••••••••••••••••••••••

My intention for today is

____

____

Re-Frame The Problem

"The highest levels of performance come to people who are centered, intuitive, creative, and reflective – people who know to see a problem as an opportunity."
~ Deepak Chopra

People need each other. I learned this after years and years of trying to run the various chapters of my life and business all by myself. My unconscious programming kept telling me that nobody was as perfect at running my business as I was, so I would let nobody help. Then one day, I realized that I was a problem. I had exceeded my own ability to grow the company by trying to do it all. My mindful meditation practice guided me to realize that my problem was an opportunity to employ other people. Today, reflect on where you are, where you have been, and where you want to go. That one thing you fear is your greatest point of opportunity. Begin to reframe the problem into possibility.

October 23

My intention for today is

____

____

Believe = Be-a-live

"Don't look for your dreams to come true; look to become true to your dreams." ~ Michael Bernard Beckwith

In my keynote talks, I often play with words. As we talked about back in March, I find it fascinating how the word believe with just a minor change can become be-live. And beliefs are, after all, how you are being with your life. If your dream was your true life, how would you step up into, and believe that, about yourself? In alignment is power.

October 24

My intention for today is

____

____

Childhood Wisdom Welcomed

"You have brains in your head. You have feet in your shoes. You can steer yourself any direction you choose."
~ Dr. Seuss

As I was collecting the inspirations for this book, I invited many friends, colleagues, and family members to share what inspires them in tough times. I loved seeing quotes from politicians, authors, artists, and more flow in. What I found in so many of them was a childlike wonder. Dr. Seuss nailed it with this inspiration. The longer we sit in applied mindfulness practice, sometimes the deeper or more difficult we think it needs to be. Yet wisdom can be simple. Put another way: pray and move your feet. Today, pray and move your feet in the direction you choose.

October 25

My intention for today is

____

____

Affirm the Good

"Let us think only of the good days that are to come."
~ Agatha Christie

Remember back in April, we dedicated the entire month to positive affirmation statements. These were not fancy quotes spouted by famous people, but simple words – short statements to reprogram our minds to the possible and the positive in our world. What you think about, you bring about. Today, flip back through April, find an affirmation that speaks to your heart, and repeat it 70 times. Only good is coming your way. I affirm it as so.

October 26

My intention for today is

____

____

Act From Spirit

"Vision without action is just a dream, action without vision just passes the time, and vision with action can change the world." ~ Nelson Mandela

You have your authentic vision for life. You have been working with your vision over time and taking daily action in setting your intentions. Some things are probably moving; others are probably not. Today, try the practice of mindful letter writing. Select one area or situation in your life where you would like to feel change. I trust there is a person, place, or thing standing in the way. Sit down and write a letter to this person explaining what you would like to see happen. Vision yourself sending the letter (but DON'T send it). Merely doing this action will open a connection to the world for that which you want to have happen to happen. Act from your Spirit, and watch the thing you want to change move. It may be slight, but it will move.

October 27

My intention for today is

____

____

Creating Perfect Timings

"Change your life today. Don't gamble on the future, act now, without delay." ~ Simone de Beauvoir

Many people think of time as either an ally or an enemy. What if I told you that time does not really exist? It is, in fact, a human construct. Is there a call you need to make, a decision that needs to be conveyed? It's a dance. Do you act now, or wait? When I find myself in these situations, I will go within and ask, "What is mine to do in this moment?" or "Do I speak up now or wait?" As you practice this over and over, your answers will get clearer. Sometimes, it's "yes"; other times, it's "no." As you follow your inner timekeeper, it will never lead you to delay. It will create for you perfect timing in all things.

October 28

My intention for today is

____

____

Balance In The Becoming

"The trick is to combine your waking rational abilities with the infinite possibilities of your dreams. Because, if you can do that, you can do anything." ~ Waking Life

I have spent many years of my life in spiritual study. In 2016 when I graduated with advanced degrees and licensure in spirituality and mindfulness, I was ready to take on the world. One problem with that was that I had shifted my world too much to heart, and I was not balanced with the head. This quote reminds us of the importance of head and heart. Today, find your own personal balance. The path to wherever you want to go is forged one thing at a time. Do one thing today to keep yourself in head and heart balance.

October 29

My intention for today is

____

____

Climb the Rope, Or Not

"Let go, or be dragged." ~ Unknown

I still remember it like it was yesterday, when my middle school gym teacher required us all to climb the rope. I was mortified. I had no interest in climbing up a rope only to have to slide back down. I mean...really, what's the point? From that day forward, I hated all thoughts of gyms, working out, or exercise. What story or experience are you dragging around with you that may no longer be serving you? Let it go and see what new story you can create. Me...I'm letting go of the rope, the climb, and the fear of exercise. I trust that new adventures will come my way.

October 30

My intention for today is

____

____

Stand For You

"To live is to choose. But to choose well, you must know who you are and what you stand for, where you want to go and why you want to get there." ~ Kofi Annan

You can't not choose. Even choosing to do or not to do is a choice in itself. As you go through this day, look at all the choices you make. Some are quick and easy choices. Others require more time and research. The key to living in a crazy world is connecting to your intuition with each choice you make. Let that still small voice inside you help choose, and you will never go wrong.

October 31

My intention for today is

____

____

Mirror Mirror On The Wall

"Kids are great imitators. Let's give them something great to imitate." ~ Anonymous

Remember those moments when you said something, and then you heard a kid repeating exactly the same thing? Why is it those memories are never of words you actually want to hear kids say? Funny life! It mirrors back to us exactly what we put out in the world. Today, put out something positive, say something kind, or send positive feelings into a meeting room, and let the world mirror back to you only positive things.

November

Gratitude and Thanksgiving

We have so much to be thankful for everyday. Yet, we don't always remember to stay in appreciation and gratefulness. These quotes, stories, and remembrances are chosen to help you fuel each day with gratitude for everything around you.

November 01

My intention for today is

____

____

Live First, Work Second

"Never confuse having a career with having a life."
~ Eddie Bauer

To fully take in this quote, you must define the word "career." A career is an occupation that is undertaken for a significant period of a person's life, where one has opportunity to advance. Today, many people will have seven or more careers. Employers no longer have the longevity of 30 plus years with the same company, as was the case in my father's generation. We are shifting the consciousness, the awareness that building a life is as important as building a career. You, and only you, can define what balance you seek in terms of careeer/work/life integration or balance. Eddie Bauer was a lover of the outdoors who, in 1920, started the sports and outdoors shop Eddie Bauer. He blended purpose and passion. How will you choose to blend your purpose and passion?

November 02

My intention for today is

____

____

Expectation vs. Expectancy

"Carry out random acts of kindness with no expectation of reward, safe in the knowledge that one day someone might do the same for you." ~ Diana, Princess of Wales

It's not that hard to be kind to people. Here are eight ways I try to be kind each day that do not take much time or money:

- Open the door for someone
- Smile as you walk by
- Pick up litter
- Share a compliment with someone
- Leave change at a vending machine
- Let a car go in front of you
- Share an inspirational quote from this book with someone
- Donate your unused items to charity

So often, when you expect to get something back, you set yourself up to be disappointed. When you do something without expectancy – simply with the energy of knowing that when you give good, good will eventually come to you – you make the world a better place.

November 03

My intention for today is

____

____

National Day of Kindness

"It is easy to be kind." ~ Karin Snyder

Today, spend your mindful moments recognizing that it is easy to be kind. Repeat to yourself: "May I be happy, healthy, peaceful, and free from suffering, and may my actions in some way contribute to the happiness, health, peace, and freedom for all." If you want to live in a kind world, be kind to yourself. Keep it simple. Smile at each person who walks by, hold open a door, pick up the trash, make a small donation to charity.

November 04

My intention for today is

____

____

Help One Another

"If there is at least one person you've helped in life, then your life has been worthwhile." ~ L. Sydney Abel

During the month of November, we hear a lot about gratitude and thanksgiving. Incidentally, the things we often are the most thankful for are, in fact, things. Our car, home, clothing, books, technology. Yet it is the people in our lives who should receive our greatest gratitude. Today, give thanks for the people you have been able to help in this life and the people who have helped you.

November 05

My intention for today is

____

____

Share You With Our World

"You give but little when you give of your possessions. It is when you give of yourself you truly give."
~ Kahlil Gibran

Many people seeking the highest levels of purpose and meaning in life take classes on abundance and prosperity. These are two words that can often get a little confusing. Abundance is the truth of all that is around us. Our world is, by nature, abundant – having plenty. Today, feel into your abundance. What do you have that you can share?

November 06

My intention for today is

____

____

Rise!

"You will never rise to your greatest potential by being all things to all people." ~ Sally Hogshead

In this quote, we find one of the hardest lessons in mindful living – practicing each day to be in the present moment, to be kind to ourselves. It feels counterproductive to recognize that you cannot be all things to all people. Today, ask yourself what is mine to do? What is NOT mine to do? Do the things your intuition tells you to do, let go of the things it tells you not to do. Trust that you will be what you need to be to the people you are here to serve, and the rest will work itself out.

November 07

My intention for today is

____

____

Crack To Let The Light In

"The wound is the place where the Light enters you."
~ Rumi

Our world can be cruel. It can be harsh. We often break. It is what we do in the broken times that shows us our new path to the light. Today, honor your cracks and the cracks in others. Allow light to come in.

November 08

My intention for today is

____

____

Approaching a Tunnel

"The cave you fear to enter holds the treasure that you seek." ~ Joseph Campbell

When you drive and come upon a tunnel, what thoughts go through your mind? Are you excited about the wonder found within, or a little less than excited about the darkness you are about to enter? There is no right or wrong answer here, and it may actually be a metaphor for how you live your life. A cave is similar to a tunnel in that it invites you into excitement and darkness. Go where you are fearful and find the treasures within.

November 09

My intention for today is

____

____

Fill Your Cup: Harvest Your Good

"Accept what life offers you and try to drink from every cup. All wines should be tasted; some should only be sipped, but with others, drink the whole bottle."
~ Paulo Coelho

Where in your life are you only taking sips of your good, when you should be drinking it in? Where are you gulping the bad where you should be sipping? Living a mindful live is knowing we have access to all good, but we have only a plate or a glass to serve it on. Today, look at what you have on your plate or in your glass. Give thanks for it, and decide how you want to consume and harvest more good for the rest of the year.

November 10

My intention for today is

____

____

Volunteer Victories

"I believe that every human mind feels pleasure in doing good to one another." ~ Thomas Jefferson

Few people realize that I built my early career around volunteerism. Upon reflection, I have built all of my careers on volunteering. I call them volunteer victories – opportunities to give to the world. It is natural sometimes to have down days. But today, and every day, if you focusing on doing good for someone else, I know it will make you feel better.

November 11

My intention for today is

____

____

11:11

"Synchronicity happens when you align with the flow of the universe, rather than insisting the universe flow your way." ~ Unknown

I happen to believe that everything is a sign, or nothing is. Therefore, I believe that all things are synchronistically happening for my good. I often laugh that Spirit speaks to me in vanity license plates. I can be driving around randomly and then see that the plate in front of me reads "IDREAM" or "UGOGIRL." I always take and share the photos on my social media. What do you believe about synchronicity in your life? Look around you – where are the messages around you that remind you life is good?

November 12

My intention for today is

____

____

Meet You In The Middle

"A good compromise is one where everybody makes a contribution." ~ Angela Merkel

This year, we have seen numerous debates on various issues. It has become easier to fight un-relentlessly than to find a way to compromise. In your mindful practice, when those inevitable arguments come up, pause to confirm that you and the other party are indeed arguing the same argument. I am always happy to have a debate, compromise, or conversation when we can start from a healthy place of understanding the argument and the desire for a shared solution.

November 13

My intention for today is

____

____

Nurture Yourself

"Balance is really about harmony. It is about a harmonic convergence of doing and being. It is about consciously deciding that no life is actually fulfilled working all of the time. It is also not fulfilled by doing so much for others that you cannot find any room for self-nurturing."
~ Cynthia James

Every day, it seems that we are trying to restore our personal self balance and harmony moment to moment. In a human-created world where we are pulled off balance at any given moment, one of the keys to balance and harmony is to find ways to nurture yourself. It used to be that self care consisted of long walks on the beach and spa days. That may no longer be true or realistic. Today, find two ways to nurture yourself in less than five minutes. Here are a few ideas: truly stop and enjoy your coffee, take a short mindful walk to the car making sure to fully feel your feet on the ground, smell a flower, listen to a whole song on the radio while doing nothing else. Nurture yourself. There is, after all, only one you.

November 14

My intention for today is

____

____

YES!!

"N-O is my new yes
When I say 'no,' I'm saying 'yes' to me.
N-O is my new yes
When I say 'no,' I set myself free."
~ Karen Drucker

It's November – what a great month to celebrate you. Say "no." You are not here on Earth to be everything to everyone. You are here to live your passion and purpose. That may mean you say "no" to someone else's purpose and passion. I have gotten better at this. "No" becomes a complete sentence the more I practice it. This November, find a few times to say "no." Then go celebrate!

November 15

My intention for today is

____

____

Lanterns For Hope

"We're here for a reason. I believe a bit of the reason is to throw little torches out to lead people through the dark." ~ Whoopie Goldberg

Luminaria are the little bags that are set up like lanterns in the fall and winter to light pathways. Sometimes, they are small candleholders with a tea light in them. Luminaria and the ceremonies around them represent hope. Our world needs hope now more than ever. Today, light a candle for yourself or be a light of hope for someone else.

November 16

My intention for today is

____

____

Power of Being Polite

"Don't mistake politeness for a lack of strength."
~ Sonya Sotomayor

Politeness is the ability to be respectful and considerate of other people. It is how you should interact with the world, courteous and civil. Politeness shows an understanding of other people's feelings. Sadly, I sense politeness is no longer taught in the same way it used to be. Having good manners should not be a lost art. Politeness is not just for the one percent. Today, one way to rekindle the lost art of politeness is say please, say thank you, and encourage harmony. This is strength. Demonstrate politeness even when the world does not.

November 17

My intention for today is

____

____

Fear Means Go!

"If you're are paralyzed with fear it's a good sign. It shows you what you have to do." ~ Steven Pressfield

Every coach has a coach. My coach consistently reminds me that I am "weird," meaning that I have a rule: stare fear in the eye and go forward anyway. Where are you experiencing fear? I celebrate that with you and for you today. This is the starting point of mindful living and overcoming chaos. Today, unpack the thoughts, "Why am I afraid of this? How is this fear helping me? How is the fear holding me? What do I want to do with this fear?" If I told you keeping the fear was no longer an option, what move would you make? Get moving.

November 18

My intention for today is

____

____

Medi-A-What? Meditation. I can't do that!

"Meditation is not about feeling a certain way. It's about feeling the way you feel." ~ Dan Harris

There is a huge misunderstanding that everyday mindfulness means everyday meditation. While that may be true for some of you, they are two different things. But meditation can certainly be used in a mindfulness practice. Today, use your practice to breathe and feel, and to honor you. Accept what you feel. Acknowledge it. If you like it, keep it. If you don't, let it go. Meditation, you can do it! Start small and let yourself simply feel the way you feel.

November 19

My intention for today is

____

____

In Pursuit of Life

"Stop chasing the money and start chasing the passion."
~ Tony Hsieh

Whenever I have a downturn in my financial life, I have to go back and look at my passion. Have I become more focused on the money and less focused on my mission? It can be hard to trust that if you do what you love, the money will come. This requires mindful, spiritually-led, and heart-driven living. Today, renew your passion, review your finances, and be open to new streams of income. Find the passion. Flow into prosperity.

November 20

....

My intention for today is

____

____

Hope Opens New Beginnings

"Even when the world throws its worst and then turns its back, there is still always hope." ~ Pittacus Lore

Happiness
Opens
Potential
Expansion

We've been reading together now for many days and months. Sometimes inspiration falls into my world in the form of acronyms, as above – H.O.P.E. Every year is an interesting journey. Each and every day, it is part of our mindful practice to keep hope alive. Today, take a moment to pause and feel hope in your heart. Remind others of the power of hope.

November 21

My intention for today is

____

____

Danger Different Ahead

"Take the risk or lose the chance." ~ Unknown

Our world has this great concept, "risk management," that you can get entire degrees in. The whole idea makes me laugh. It is not really possible to "manage" anything. We can only choose to "lead" it. Somewhere, in your life today you face a choice – to stay safe or to risk. Yes, you can make a pro/con list and analyze the choice from every angle with your head. But today, take a new approach. Ask your inner self, your heart voice, what to do with all the data. Do you have the courage to act from what it tells you? Live intuitively, and it will be different ahead.

November 22

My intention for today is

____

____

Home Sweet Home

"Be grateful for the home you have, knowing that at this moment, all you have is all you need."
~ Sarah Ban Breathnach

A house, the building for human habitation. A home, a place where one lives. As with many things in life today, the definition of a "home" has changed and who lives at home is changing.

No matter where you live, work, play, and have your life, celebrate it today. I guarantee you, someone has a home that you perceive as "better," but they are not happy. Someone else has something you perceive as "less," but they are not happy. Happiness comes when you are grateful in the home exactly where you are.

November 23

My intention for today is

____

____

Simply Positive

"The principle of positive thinking is simplicity itself. Picture an outcome, dwell on it in your thoughts and feelings, and unseen agencies—whether metaphysical or psychological—will supposedly come to your aid. Seen in this way, the mind is a causative force."
~ Mitch Horowitz

Your thoughts are the seeds of the life you create. Are you anticipating grief or joy? Are you looking back with fear or happiness? No matter where you look, the stories you tell – both positive and negative – make up the life you are currently living and the life you are creating. While some people think of me as "Holly-anna Polly-anna," I'll take that positive affirmation and the positive life that comes with it. Today, picture an outcome you desire. Plant that as a seed each day, and watch positivity grow for you and for those around you.

November 24

My intention for today is

____

____

A Day of Giving

"A gift is pure when it is given from the heart to the right person at the right time and at the right place, and when we expect nothing in return."
~ Anonymous, The Bhagavad Gita

Circulation is key to living without stress and chaos. When you believe that what you give comes back to you, you become more careful about what you give out. Give out kindness. Get kindness. Give its opposite, and look what comes back to you. The National Day of Giving takes place in November. Find one thing in your heart you would like to circulate. Give it away with no strings attached.

November 25

My intention for today is

____

____

FOCUS

"Win or lose, you will never regret working hard, making sacrifices, being disciplined or focusing too much."
~ John Smith

First
Open
Conscious
Universal
Spirit

Today's acronym links the need for focus with the balance of flow. Today open your consciousness, thoughts, stories, words, and ideas to the universal good flowing all around. When good is all you see around you, the sacrifices melt to success. The disciplined melts to delight. And the focus is fantastic connection to your highest self.

November 26

My intention for today is

____

____

Gratitude Expands Your Truth

"Gratitude is riches. Complaint is poverty." ~ Doris Day

I grew up in a trailer park. This upbringing often makes my default setting: I grew up "poor." As I do my mindfulness practice today, I am consistently resetting my mindset to remember that every complaint comes from lack. Truth is, while my address may have been a trailer park, I grew up in a very loving household. The shift to gratitude has allowed me to be wealthy. For what are you grateful today? Expand your riches.

November 27

My intention for today is

____

____

Challenging Teachers

"Your best teacher is the person offering you your greatest challenge." ~ Cheryl Richardson

Relationships. Our greatest teaching tool. In fact, most of our best teachers in life are not the teachers we come into contact with in a traditional or online classroom. The teacher we often need most is the co-worker, child, spouse, or friend. Or the grocery store clerk or coffee shop barista. We are all teachers to one another, whether we want to be or not. As you look through your Facebook friend list or Rolodex, or simply at the list of people you will come into contact with today, ask yourself, "Who makes my emotions hot?" That person is your teacher. Ask your inner wisdom self, that voice inside, what they are here to teach you? Listen. Are you ready to learn the lesson?

November 28

My intention for today is

____

____

Directionally Challenged

"Confusion is when the head says go left, and the heart says go right." ~ JD Messenger

I often wish my head and heart could get it together. Can you relate? Over the years of my mindfulness practice, I have found that in moments of confusion, the best thing I can do is keep asking for guidance and clarity. Today, if you have a "recalculating" moment, don't be in a hurry to decide. Let the answers come naturally.

November 29

My intention for today is

____

____

Point of No Return

"From a certain point onward there is no turning back. That is the point that must be reached." ~ Franz Kafka

The process of being human has natural "no return" moments. For example, graduating from high school or college. Getting married or divorced. The choice to have kids or not. While all three of these examples have different magnitudes and options, they are turning points. In numerology, we learn there are cycles of seven, eight, or nine years that we move through in our lives. If you are at one of these moments, or another one, celebrate it! Accept it! The Universe has your back. Allow the old to flow out, and the new to flow in.

November 30

My intention for today is

____

____

Chaos & Fractals

"In all chaos there is a cosmos, in all disorder a secret order." ~ Carl Jung

As a young student, I studied chaos theory and fractals. On one level, this is the study of how we are connected. When a butterfly flaps its wings in China, how does that shift energy around the world? We live in an ever-ending feedback loop. Today, reflect on and study how you are self-similar – how we are all moving through chaos, and yet, there is still order in it.

December

Decide

It seems each passing year goes faster than the last. Did we not just begin this everyday mindfulness journey? Thank you for being a part of shifting the planet from mindless chaos to mindful calm. Your choice and commitment make a difference in your life and the lives of those around you. Our December theme is decide. May these quotes and stores help you to mindfully make choices each day that support you in health, wealth, happiness, and dreams.

December 01

My intention for today is

____

____

Define Holiday

As the energy of the planet shifts into "holiday mode," I want you to take this day to define for yourself what this holiday season will be about. My name is Holly, for goodness sake. Everyone thinks I am a "December baby," but that is not true. Instead of a me providing a quote today, I want to invite you to find a quote of your own that will ground your holiday season. Feel free to send it to me at listen@EverydayMindfulnessShow.com. Who knows, we may use it on a December show to inspire us all!

December 02

My intention for today is

____

____

I Love My Life

"I choose to make the rest of my life the best of my life."
~ Louise Hay

What is your intention for today? What is one word or a short statement that will set energy in motion this day? December is often one of the hardest months to stay on track. I open this month with a friendly reminder: your words create your month. What are you creating? Choose to make this month the best ever.

December 03

My intention for today is

____

____

Courage of the Heart

"We can know only that we know nothing. And that is the highest degree of human wisdom." ~ Leo Tolstoy

Breathe in Nothing. Breathe out Nothing.

Do this until you feel only openness. Let wisdom flow into that space. Today, have the courage to open your heart to know nothing. Ask someone a question, come from a place of not knowing, and see how the answer will fill you.

December 04

My intention for today is

____

____

Choose To Go One More Step

"It is our choices, Harry, that show what we truly are, far more than our abilities." ~ Albus Dumbledore

Just because you are able to do something does not mean that you will. I am able to unload the dishwasher. It does not mean that I will. Today, look at all your talents and abilities. You are able to do a lot of things. What will you choose to do with your talents, gifts, and abilities on this day? What you choose to do with each day becomes what you choose to do with your life. You have one life, so make mindful choices what to do with it.

December 05

. . . .

My intention for today is

____

____

Anticipatory Worry

"Worry is a prayer to chaos." ~ Gabrielle Bernstein

I often laugh when the countdown to Christmas often starts the day after Halloween. This is anticipatory worry – putting out into the conscious mind that which you do not want to have happen. Today, spend a few moments in anticipatory joy. Turn chaos into anticipation. What joy do you anticipate this holiday season?

December 06

My intention for today is

____

____

Question Everything, Then Decide

"You create your life in two ways: by the statements you say to yourself and others, and by the questions you ask yourselves and others." ~ Noah St. John

What if you changed your affirmations for questions? In his work, Noah St. John invites us to do that and, in so doing, open the universe up to respond. Today, think about what you are affirming for yourself and make it a question. For example, "I am making $5,000 this month" is the affirmation. The question is "How am I am I making $5,000 this month?" I use this practice often, and I am mindfully amazed at what happens as the universe answers my questions.

December 07

My intention for today is

____

____

History Reminder

"Yesterday, December 7th, 1941, a date which will live in infamy, the United States of America was suddenly and deliberately attacked by naval and air forces of the Empire of Japan." ~ Franklin D. Roosevelt

In Everyday Mindfulness, I have intentionally avoided references to history. Mindfulness is, after all, the practice of being in this moment. So in this moment, as you read this historical quote, what is it here to teach you today? Where are you deliberately attacking yourself? Is there something in history still holding you back as we enter the holiday season? Can you honor this history, but write a new story?

December 08

....

My intention for today is

____

____

Understand It First

"To fix any problem, you must first understand it."
~ Christy Lamagna

Life is expanded when you ask more mindful questions. You may have noticed that many of the pages of this guide contain questions to connect you to you, and you to others.

Whatever challenge you face today, seek to understand it deeper.

December 09

My intention for today is

____

____

Spirit Is Found in Balance

"There is no decision we can make that doesn't come with some sort of balance or sacrifice." ~ Simon Sinek

Our December theme is decide. Your mindful choices are decisions about how you will create this holiday season. As you choose one thing over others, bless and release the other choices you are not making during this busy time. While we can't be in two places at the same time, we can bless where we are and also where we can't be – as it is all expanding the good in the world.

December 10

My intention for today is

____

____

Guilt Over Obligation

"December 25th has become guilt and obligation."
~ Phil Donahue

No matter what holiday tradition you are celebrating, pause today and look at what decisions you are making out of obligation. What decisions are you making because they serve you and your intention for today? Release obligation, receive the fa la la! It is the happiest time of the year after all.

December 11

My intention for today is

____

____

Friendly or Hostile

"The most important decision we make is whether we believe we live in a friendly or hostile universe."
~ Albert Einstein

As you start this day, pause and really ask your heart, "Do I believe in a friendly or unfriendly world?" Is the world for you, or against you? Envision every plan you have today – every meeting, experience, person, place, or thing – and sense that they are friendly to you and you to them. Tonight or tomorrow, reflect on how this activity may have created a more friendly day.

December 12

My intention for today is

____

____

12 Days of Christmas

"The truth creates an opening." ~ Danielle LaPorte

A few years back, I started a fun tradition I call the 12 Days of Holiday Socks. I mean with a name like Holly, you can imagine I have quite the holiday collection. This silly little tradition created an opening. I post photos of the socks on my various social media platforms. Over the years, the socks bring smiles to people's faces and have become a tradition they look forward to. Lots of people send me socks now. The truth is, little things connect us. Little things create light, energy, and openings. Today, ask yourself, "What is a way I can stand in my truth and create an opening?"

December 13

My intention for today is

____

____

Choose You

"In essence, you make your choices, and then your choices make you." ~ Darren Hardy

Tap into your feelings today. Pause. Breathe. Feel. Repeat. Your feelings come from your choices. Are you choosing to feel in supportive ways or in ways that are unsupportive? Make a choice today that makes you your best self.

December 14

My intention for today is

____

____

Pursue Your Dream

"All our dreams can come true, if we have courage to pursue them." ~ Walt Disney

December brings out the childlike wonder in many of us. What was one of your childhood dreams? It's never too late. Invite the core of your heart to share with you that child wish that is still wanting to be realized. Look for ways to make it come true.

December 15

My intention for today is

____

____

Do Different! Do You!

"I was motivated to be different in part because I was different." ~ Donna Brazille

Each day looks a little different to each one of us. Even if you wake up in the same house, drive the same commute, and do the same work, your experience of the day will be different from anyone else's. So why is it that we automatically assume the person sitting next to us is having the same experience? They are not. Today, honor your view of the world, your practice, thoughts, views, and choices that make you you. Do you! Honor the different of the person next to you, also.

December 16

My intention for today is

____

____

Travel At The Holidays

"Travel is the only thing you buy that makes you richer."
~ Anonymous

If you want to see a world that really needs a mindfulness practice, travel during a holiday. Everyone is checking more luggage, running late, and a little nervous about being with family. Today, use your mindfulness practice to support someone else. Use travel – be it walking, driving, train or plane – when someone comes to you frazzled, panicked, or upset. Remind them to breathe. Pause and invite them to breathe out the stress with you.

December 17

My intention for today is

____

____

Make Time For Friends

"You and I are a team. Nothing is more important than our friendship." ~ Monsters, Inc.

We have re-defined the word friend with the advent of Facebook Friends. From time to time, I'll hear someone say that they have 5,000 friends. Then when you ask them what is really going on, they are lonely. The holidays can be a lonely time for some. Offer your friendship to someone today. Nothing will be more remembered at the holidays than the gift of your thoughtful time.

December 18

My intention for today is

____

____

Avert Crisis Pro-Act

"If we all looked out for each other a little bit more, I think we wouldn't have a lot of the crisis that we have in today's society." ~ Criss Angel

It used to be said, "It takes a village to raise a child." Today, it's more like, "How dare you say anything to my child!" I find the holidays to be a time when we can look out for one another a little more. Today, check in on a friend.

December 19

My intention for today is

____

____

Be Nice

"It's nice to be important, but it's important to always be nice." ~ Alyssa Milano

Nice is a word that sadly we don't hear as often as we used to. To be nice means to be enjoyable, pleasant, delightful. Today, how can you be nice? Find someone you may not have been nice to, and find a way to be nice.

December 20

My intention for today is

____

____

See The Best In Everything

"Not having the best situation, but seeing the best in your situation is the key to happiness." ~ Marie Forleo

Where are you frustrated today? Where is something in your world not going right? Use that as an opportunity to activate today's inspirational quote. See the best in the situation, and choose to be happy.

December 21

My intention for today is

____

____

Present Presence

"If you are not fully PRESENT, how will you notice the PRESENTS the universe has set aside for you?"
~ Raj Setty

Next, next, next...this is often how the holidays go. Run from one event to the next. Today, as you make transitions from each event, walk slowly and feel your feet on the ground. Give yourself moments to be present.

December 22

My intention for today is

____

____

Circulate Love

"For it is in the giving that we receive." ~ Francis of Assisi

This time of year, we can become mindless very easily – lost in the hustle and bustle of getting everything done. We get so focused on the "giving" list that we forget the ultimate purpose of giving. Pause today and see the bounty that is already all around you. Smell a tree, take in a light, look a salesperson in the eye. Remember, when you give, you also receive.

December 23

My intention for today is

____

____

Act in Love

"Christmas, my child, is love in action. Every time we love, every time we give, it's Christmas." ~ Dale Evans

While not every reader of this book celebrates Christmas, I trust every reader celebrates the act of giving. As we have talked about before, there is often a forgotten double side to giving: receiving. Today, put love in action by consciously receiving.

December 24

My intention for today is

____

____

Kindness Is

"What I regret most in my life are the failures of kindness." ~ George Saunders

There are many references to kindness in this book. Kindness is something we must activate each day for ourselves first, so we can then activate that kindness for others. On the eve of this holiday, how can you find one place to be kind to yourself and one place to be kind for the world around you?

December 25

My intention for today is

____

____

Mind Your Feelings & Feel Your Mind This Christmas

"Christmas, children is not a date. It is a state of mind."
~ Mary Ellen Chase

With the name Holly, most people assume, wrongly, that I am a holiday baby. This is a reminder that we often make assumptions. Some people assume that Christmas is the best day of the year. It can actually be a challenge for many people. Today, remember your mindset creates the day. Whether you are celebrating around a tree with family or feeling sad while missing someone, set an intentional mindset today that supports you. What present will you give yourself today?

December 26

My intention for today is

____

____

Wanting & Getting

"You don't necessarily get what you want, but you should want what you get." ~ Carolyn Strauss

The day after Christmas is the biggest retail return shopping day of the year. What a sad state of the world where we can be so ungrateful that we immediately return the well intentioned, and in some cases well-thought-out, gifts from loved ones. Look at all the gifts in your life, not simply those exchanged at the holidays. You have so much to be grateful for.

December 27

My intention for today is

____

____

Fireside Warmth

"What good is warmth without cold to give it sweetness?" ~ John Steinbeck

Nothing is better on a cold winter day than a fire. Fire is an essential element of life. Today, light a candle, start a fire (if you can), and feel the warmth warm you.

December 28

My intention for today is

____

____

Risk It & Accept the Reward

"Risk is the price you pay for opportunity." ~ Tom Selleck

As this year comes to a close, take a moment to reflect on what risks you took this year. What were the rewards of these risks? As you begin to consider the trajectory you want for your life going forward, what reward do you seek? Are you willing to step up to the risk?

December 29

My intention for today is

____

____

Let Life Happen

"If you talk about it, it's a dream,
if you envision it, it's possible,
but if you schedule it, it's real."
~ Anthony Robbins

As another year is about to come and go, don't mourn what is behind. Look ahead and celebrate what is yet to be. Motivational speaker Anthony Robbins had a very challenging upbringing that he now shares as fuel for inspiring others. No matter what you are here to become – parent, teacher, doctor, construction worker, or a new career yet to be created– it's time to make it real. The world is waiting.

December 30

My intention for today is

____

____

There Is a Power In Silence

"Learn to get in touch with the silence within yourself, and know that everything in life has purpose."
~ Elisabeth Kubler-Ross

What a year you have journeyed with me. A mindfulness practice is a personal choice that often takes place in the still, small, quiet moments. While we have celebrated together 365 days of inspirational quotes and anecdotes, always remember: mindful matters and so do you.

December 31

••••••••••••••••••••••••

My intention for today is

____

____

Endings & Beginnings

"Leap beyond history into a new story."
~ Elizabeth Lesser

I am a huge reader. You may be also. There is that sad moment when you come to realize the book is ending. I find this is equally true when I come to the end of a blank journal. Today, it's time to leap to your new story.